Getting Started in
Project
Management

Paula Martin
and
Karen Tate

John Wiley & Sons, Inc.

New York • Chichester • Weinheim • Brisbane • Singapore • Toronto

This book is printed on acid-free paper. ∞

Published by John Wiley & Sons, Inc.
Published simultaneously in Canada.

This publication is designed to provide accurate and authoritative information in regard to the subject matter covered. It is sold with the understanding that the publisher is not engaged in rendering professional services. If professional advice or other expert assistance is required, the services of a competent professional person should be sought.

Library of Congress Cataloging-in-Publication Data:
Martin, Paula.
    Getting started in project management / by Paula Martin and Karen Tate.
        p.   cm.
    Includes index.
    ISBN 0-471-13503-8 (pbk. : alk. paper)
    1. Project management.   I. Tate, Karen.   II. Title.
HD69.P75 M377 2001
658.4'04—dc21   2001026851

Printed in the United States of America.

10 9 8 7 6 5 4 3 2 1

Getting Started in
Project
Management

The Getting Started In Series

Contents

About the Authors

Paula K. Martin and Karen Tate, PMP are the co-founders of MartinTate, a project management training and consulting company with headquarters in Cincinnati, Ohio. They are also the authors of the *Project Management Memory Jogger™*, a best-selling pocket guide to project management, and columnists for the Project Management Institute's magazine, *PM Network*.

MartinTate is the leading provider of team-based, project management training. Their clients include GE Capital, the Internal Revenue Service, Global One, Ernst & Young, United Nations, Wyett-Ayerst Pharmaceutical, the City of Seattle, Corning Precision Lens, and other organizations in all parts of the world.

Paula Martin, CEO of MartinTate, is also the author of: *Executive Guide: The 7 Keys to Project Success*, a book for managers on how to create successful projects across the organization; *A Step by Step Approach to Risk Assessment*, a how-to book for project leaders; *Leading Project Management into the 21st Century*, a book for managers on how to create a project friendly environment; *Project Sabotage*, a business mystery novel about project management; and *The Buck Stops Here: Accountability and the Empowered Manager*, a book on vertical management and the new accountability.

Ms. Martin has been consulting on project management, matrix management, project steering, management accountability, and other key leadership issues for over 10 years. Prior to becoming a consultant she was the director of American Cyanamid's new product development efforts in the United States, steering hundreds of projects and project teams. Paula is a frequent presenter at project management conferences around the world.

Karen Tate, PMP, President of MartinTate, is a certified Project Management Professional (PMP)® from the Project Management Institute. She is the co-author of *Triz: An Approach to Systematic Innovation*.

Ms. Tate has been working with projects and project teams for more than 20 years. Prior to forming her own consulting business, Karen was a project manager in two worldwide consulting firms, working directly with multiple customers at all levels, where she managed programs and projects of all types and sizes, in a variety of industries. Currently she teaches project management to teams of all types and sizes in organizations around the world.

Ms. Tate also serves on the Education Advisory Group of the Project Management Institute, an internationally recognized project management association.

Introduction

S o you're new to project management. Well, you're not alone. Lots of people are discovering that project management is a tool that can help make their projects more successful. You've probably been doing projects for a long time: projects at work—such as developing a new product, improving a process, implementing a new service—and projects at home—such as planning a wedding or a family reunion. Family vacations and fund–raising events are also projects.

For many people, working on a project is a frustrating experience. Team members can't agree on what should be done or how to do it. Deadlines are missed. The customer is unhappy. Morale is poor. It doesn't have to be this way. Projects can be both fun and successful, if you use an effective method for helping you work through the steps of the project. And that's just what you're going to get when you read this book: a simple, easy-to-use method for managing any project.

The CORE Project Management™ method that you'll learn will help improve the results for all your projects. All you need to do is follow the yellow brick road through the steps we'll discuss and apply them to a project you're working on. Voilá. Your project is better organized, you're more successful, and you're having fun. It doesn't get much better than that.

WHAT IS IN THIS BOOK?

This book is organized in the order of the steps you'll use to manage your project. Fortunately projects are mostly linear—they have a beginning, a middle, and an end—so a book, which is also linear, lends itself well to walking you through the steps you'll need to create great projects.

✔ **Chapter 1. The Basics.** Learn the basic characteristics of a project and how projects differ from the normal way that work gets done. Discover why you should be using the new approach to project management instead of the old approach. Explore the types of people who typically work on projects and what the role of each should be. Finally, learn the four phases of any project and what's required in each phase if you're going to create a successful project.

✔ **Chapter 2. Initiating a Project.** Discover what each section of the charter, the document that starts or initiates a project, should contain. Learn how to complete a charter. Set up an issues list and a lessons-learned list, in preparation for the next project phase, and assemble your project team.

✔ **Chapter 3. Leading the Project Team.** Projects are done through people and part of the role of the project leader is leading the team. Learn the key principles for leading teams and why team participation in the project management process is so important. Then walk through the five stages of team development to discover how to create a high performing team. Finally, assess your own skills as a project leader.

✔ **Chapter 4. Kicking Off the Project.** The kick-off meeting is when the team is assembled for the first time and they're introduced to the project. It sets the tone for the rest of the project. Learn how to conduct a kick-off meeting the right way. Walk through a sample agenda of what to do and how to do it.

✔ **Chapter 5. Planning the Scope.** The scope defines what will be done by the project. Planning the scope sets the stage for everything else that happens in the project, so it's important to do it right. Discover how to set an appropriate target for your project. Learn how to recognize the different types of customers and to define the customer's need appropriately.

✔ **Chapter 6. Organizing the Project.** Learn the right way to break a project down into manageable pieces and how to organize those pieces into chunks of work that can be assigned to someone on the team. Explore the composition of the team to make sure you've included the right people and learn what is required to effectively empower a team.

✔ **Chapter 7. Assessing Risk.** Problems occur in every project. The key to keeping chaos at bay is preventing as many of the problems from occurring as possible. As we review the risk assessment process we'll answer a number of questions: Who should be invited to the risk assessment meeting? What's the best way to identify risks? How can the risks be analyzed after they have been identified? How can the risks be avoided, if possible?

✔ **Chapter 8. Developing a Schedule.** Every project needs a schedule; most projects need two types of schedules: one that depicts the big picture of the project, which is used to communicate the schedule to people outside the team, and one that helps the team manage the deadlines for the project. Walk through the steps of creating both types of schedules. Learn what to do if you can't meet your deadlines.

✔ **Chapter 9. Developing a Budget.** All projects consume resources and most cost money. However, not all projects require a project budget, although all projects ought to create one. Learn how to estimate costs and create a spending estimate to include in your project plan.

✔ **Chapter 10. Assembling the Plan.** After you've worked through the steps of planning, you're ready to assemble the project plan document and get it approved. Learn what should be in a project plan and how to write the executive summary. Include a process for how you'll manage changes to the plan after it's been approved.

✔ **Chapter 11. Team-Based Tools.** In addition to the project management tools that have been covered thus far, you'll need a few decision-making tools to help you get through the rest of the project. Learn how to effectively brainstorm, organize, analyze, and then make decisions on ideas or issues generated by the team.

✔ **Chapter 12. Executing the Plan.** After the plan is approved, it's time to get to work. However, as you complete the work, it's important to continually monitor the progress of the project to make sure it stays on track. You'll also need to continually assess the environment to determine if any new risks have popped up that weren't anticipated in the risk assessment.

✔ **Chapter 13. Closing Out the Project.** You're almost there. You've finished the work and you're ready to disband. But wait! You still need to evaluate the customer's satisfaction, summarize the lessons that were learned throughout the course of the project, and assemble a close-out report. Then, it's time to celebrate. Congratulations. You're done!

✔ **Chapter 14. Summing Up.** Review the key elements of effective team participation and the seven keys to success for any project.

Project management is a process, like a journey down the yellow brick road. We'll walk through the steps of project management together, discovering new territory, melting any fears and solving problems you've experienced in the past, revisiting old haunts, and, finally, making it to the emerald city of greater project success.

Project management isn't just for project managers anymore. If you're not a project manager, but you're aspiring to be one or you're working on a project team and want to do a better job, this book is for you. What are we waiting for? We've just crash-landed in Munchkin land and it's time to get moving.

Chapter 1

The Basics

WHAT IS A PROJECT?

Before we can begin our journey through the land of project management, we need to cover a few basics. The first question we need to address is what exactly is a project? For example, is building a custom house a project? What if you're a developer and you have a crew that builds a standard house over and over again? Is that a project? The first example, the custom house, is a project, but building the standard house is a business process. Let's examine the similarities between projects and business process:

- ✔ Both turn inputs into outputs through a series of tasks or activities. In our example, these activities would include digging a foundation, framing the house, roofing, and so on.
- ✔ Both produce outputs or products when they are completed. The output of the project is a custom house. The outputs of the business process are standard houses.

Obviously, projects and business processes are not the same thing. Let's examine the differences:

7

First, building a single custom house is a temporary event, not a repetitive one. You build one house and then you're done. If you continually build houses, then the process of house building is repeated each time a house is built. Second, when you build a custom house, the output is unique. There's no other house exactly like it. When you build standard houses, each one is basically the same. Third, if you build one house, you pull together a team of subcontractors and assign them tasks to do. If your business is building standard houses, you already have plumbers, electricians, carpenters, and other crafts people on staff who work on one house and then move on to the next. (See Table 1.1.)

Let's look at another example. What if you were to design and install a new process for ordering and fulfilling products (taking the order, picking, packing, shipping)? Is that a project? Well, it's temporary; once you install the process you wouldn't be designing and installing it again. It produces a unique deliverable—a fulfillment process that is ready to run—and there are no predefined jobs for designing or installing fulfillment processes within your company. Therefore, creating a fulfillment process satisfies the criteria for a project.

What about running the order/fulfillment process once it's installed? Is that a project or is it a business process? You are going to be taking and filling orders on an ongoing basis, which means you'll be repeating the same process over and over again. And you'll get the same output each time—shipped boxes. Finally, you'll have people assigned

TABLE 1.1 Projects vs. Business Processes	
Project	*Business Process*
1. Temporary: has a beginning and an end	1. Ongoing: The same process is repeated over and over again
2. Produces a unique output or deliverable	2. Produces the same output each time the process is run
3. Has no predefined work assignments	3. Has predefined work assignments

who do the ordering and picking and packing, so, yes, the running of the order/fulfillment process is a business process.

So, if you are creating something new—a new software application or a new training program, or if you want to improve something like redesigning a process or a product or changing the way a service is delivered—you've got yourself a project. If you want to continue doing what you've done in the past, you are working in a business process. Business processes are managed using process management. Projects are managed using project management.

WHAT IS PROJECT MANAGEMENT?

Project management is a set of tools, techniques, and knowledge that, when applied, helps you produce better results for your project. Trying to manage a project without project management is like trying to play football without a game plan. The coach would get the players together and say, "How should we play this game? We're supposed to get more points than the other team and to do that we have to score goals. Now everyone go out and do what you think needs to be done in order to win."

What are the chances that the team will win? Not very high. What's missing? A game plan for how to go about winning. The coordinated execution of the game plan. A process for revising the game plan based on how the game progresses. In a project, these elements are provided by project management.

Most teams approach projects in the same way that the team described above approaches football. They get a project assignment and they start playing. Then they get together when there is a crisis and there are usually lots of them because they're playing without a game plan. When and if they ever complete the project, the team disbands, hoping never to have to repeat the experience again. Why would a team do this? First of all, they may not be aware that there is a method available that will help them to create a game plan. Secondly, they may be under the mistaken impression that creating a game plan will delay

9

the project. Not taking the time to create the plan actually increases the length of the project. When you invest in following a method, you save time overall. (See Figure 1.1.)

Project management provides you with a process that you can follow, a series of moves that will help you address some basic questions before you dive into getting the work done, questions such as what are you going to produce? What is it the customer wants and needs? Who is going to do the work? How long will it take? How much will it cost? What might go wrong? How can you avoid potential problems? These questions are addressed up front so that the work can proceed smoothly and efficiently.

In addition to helping you plan, a project management method also helps you to keep a project on track, solving problems as they

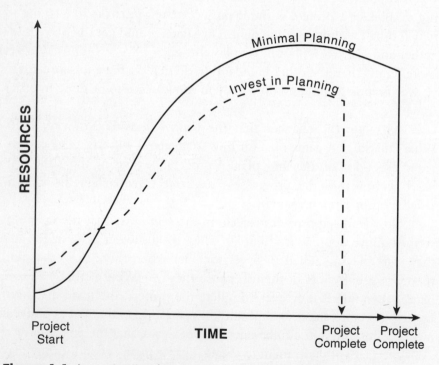

Figure 1.1 Investing in planning vs. minimal planning.

arise. It helps you manage changes that might be required for the project. For example, maybe the prospective homeowner for the custom-house project decides he or she just can't live without a screened-in porch. This requires a change to the plan. Finally, project management helps you to learn from what has happened during the project so that you can create better results for your next project.

CHARACTERISTICS OF A PROJECT MANAGEMENT METHOD

A method is a system for getting something done. If you are doing a project on your own, you can use whatever system works for you. However, when you work with a group of people, you need a common project management method because the project team must work together. There are two approaches the team could use for coming up with a method. One, they could invent one themselves, or two, they could use an already developed, proven methodology.

The value of using a proven method is that the work of developing the method has already been done for you. It's been tried and tested. That allows you to focus on what's really important—the content of the work.

The methodology we'll be discussing in this book is called the CORE Project Management™ method or CORE PM™ for short. CORE stands for:

- ✔ Collaborative—It can be used in a participatory mode with project teams.
- ✔ Open architecture—It can be used with any type of project, in any type of organization.
- ✔ Results oriented—It will help you produce successful projects that satisfy the customer.
- ✔ Easy to use—The step-by-step approach makes it easy to follow.

CORE PM was developed by the authors using the latest management technologies, such as the new accountability, total quality, theory of constraints, empowerment, teaming, and, of course, project management. Project leaders and teams all over the world, in all types of projects, have used this method. It has proven to be both easy to use and highly effective. As you'll see, it's best used in a participatory, team-based environment where the entire team is involved in planning and monitoring the project, but it can also be used by just the project leader if the project leader is planning and monitoring singlehandedly. The former is known as participatory project management and the latter as directive project management. Let's explore the differences.

DIRECTIVE PROJECT MANAGEMENT

The directive approach represents old management technology. It assumes that the project manager is the person who can do the best job of planning and controlling the project. The project manager does the planning and then delegates tasks to the team members. He or she then follows up with individual team members to make sure they are completing their tasks on time. Communication flow is primarily between the team member and the project leader. If a problem is encountered, it's up to the leader to solve it. (See Figure 1.2.)

Although the directive style is useful in some circumstances because it saves time in planning the project, it has a number of significant downsides:

✔ The whole project takes longer because the phase in which the work gets done (called execution), which is the longest phase of any project, takes longer due to confusion, misunderstandings, and rework (having to redo work because it wasn't done right the first time).

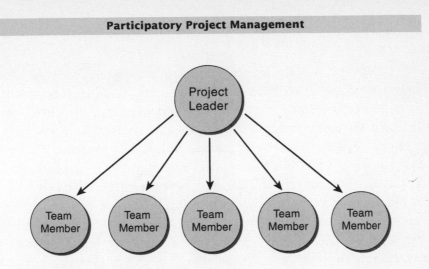

Figure 1.2 Directive style of communication.

✔ Team members have little understanding of the project as a whole or how their work fits into the big picture.

✔ There is little team ownership or commitment to the project.

PARTICIPATORY PROJECT MANAGEMENT

Participative project management represents the newer management technology for projects. The project leader facilitates the project management process, leading the team through the steps of planning. The team, under the direction of the project leader, monitors the progress of the project as the work is completed. Decisions about the work are made with the involvement of the team and communication flow is not only up and down from team members to the project leader, but across the team as well. (See Figure 1.3.)

The benefits of a participative approach are:

✔ Each member of the team understands how his or her individual piece of the project fits into the big picture.

✔ More ideas are generated.

13

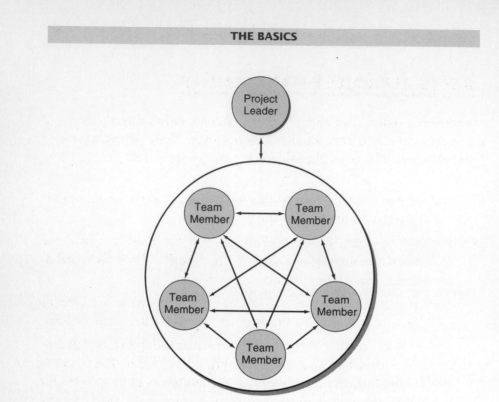

Figure 1.3 Participative style of communication.

✔ Better decisions are made when everyone participates.

✔ Participation creates ownership, which strengthens commitment and accountability.

✔ Team morale is usually higher.

✔ There is less rework.

✔ Individual and team performance is increased.

A participative approach generally provides for better project results. The CORE PM method, which we will discuss in this book, is the most widely used participative method available today.

Both directive and participative approaches depend on people. Nothing happens without the cooperation of people. Let's explore the role that people need to play in producing a successful project.

ROLES IN PROJECT MANAGEMENT

There are usually a number of people who are either directly involved in a project or who have a stake in its outcome. These people are called stakeholders. The key stakeholders in most projects are:

- ✔ Project leader—The project leader, also known as the project manager, is the head of the project.

- ✔ Project team member—Project team members produce the outputs, called deliverables, for the project. They also participate in the project management process.

- ✔ Sponsor—The sponsor is the management person who acts as a liaison between the management team and the project leader.

- ✔ Project customer—This is the person or group that will accept the final deliverable(s) that the project produces. The final deliverable is the final output and it is delivered to the project customer, whose needs and requirements are what drive the project.

- ✔ Resource managers—Resource managers, also known as functional managers, usually provide the resources, particularly the people who are involved in the project.

There may be other stakeholders as well, such as members of departments that will be impacted by the deliverables of the project. Let's examine each of the key stakeholder roles in more detail.

PROJECT LEADER ROLE

The project leader is also referred to as the project manager. However, in a participative approach, the main role for the project manager is leadership, so we refer to him or her as a project leader. The role of the project leader is to

15

✔ Provide direction to the project team.

✔ Lead the project team through the project management process (creating and executing the project plan).

✔ Obtain approvals for the project plan.

✔ Issue status reports on the progress of the project versus the plan.

✔ Respond to requests for changes to the plan.

✔ Facilitate the team process, which is the interpersonal process by which team members develop as a team.

✔ Remove obstacles for the team so they can complete the project.

✔ Act as the key interface with the project sponsor.

✔ Act as the key interface with the project customer.

✔ Call and run team meetings.

✔ Issue the final project report.

The essential role of the project leader is to lead the project team through the project management and team processes so that they complete the project successfully. The project leader is accountable for the overall success of the project.

PROJECT TEAM MEMBER

The project team member sits on the project team and is critical to the success of the project. The project team member's role is to

✔ Provide technical expertise.

✔ Provide ideas that can help the team create quality deliverables, on time and within budget.

✔ Ensure that his or her part of the project work gets completed on time.

✔ Communicate issues back to the project team.

✔ Participate in the project planning process.

✔ Interface with the suppliers for his or her area.

✔ Keep the boss informed on project issues, as required.

✔ Keep the commitment he or she makes to the project.

✔ Help to keep the project on track.

✔ Provide updates to his or her resource manager on the status of the project.

✔ Help to keep the team process and content on track.

The project team member has an active role to play in a participatory style of managing a project. The project team member not only provides technical expertise and produces deliverables, but he or she also helps in the planning and monitoring of the project. The project team member is accountable for ensuring that his or her work contributes to the overall success of the project.

SPONSOR ROLE

The sponsor is someone from management who has been designated to oversee the project, to help ensure that it satisfies both the needs of the customer and the needs of the organization. The sponsor is sometimes called the project champion.

The role of the sponsor is to

✔ Initiate the project by selecting a project leader.

✔ Make sure that the project's objectives are in line with the strategic direction/goals of the organization.

✔ Provide overall direction to the project.

✔ Make sure the team has the resources required to complete the project successfully.

✔ Obtain commitment from the resource managers to support the project.

✔ Review and approve the project plan.

✔ Review status reports.

✔ Review progress on the project with the project leader.

✔ Help to remove obstacles that can't be overcome by the team or the project leader.

✔ Mentor or coach the project leader.

✔ Review and approve the final report.

The sponsor makes sure that the project leader has the resources, training, support, and cooperation he or she needs to get the job done. The sponsor is accountable for the success of the project leader.

What happens if you don't have a sponsor? Then your boss or the project customer, if that customer is inside the organization, will need to act as the sponsor. The sponsor connects the project to the needs of management. It's very risky to start a project without one.

PROJECT CUSTOMER ROLE

A project exists to satisfy a customer. The project customer is the recipient of the main output of the project, called the final deliverable. In order to make sure the final deliverables satisfies the customer, the customer must convey to the project team what the needs and requirements for the deliverable will be.

A customer can be internal or external to the organization. Most projects are done for internal customers (customers inside the organization), although the final deliverable produced by the project might eventually be distributed to or purchased by an external customer.

Suppose you were working on a project to develop a new heart monitor for infants. The project customer is probably your marketing department because it's their job to sell the monitor to the eventual buyers, the hospitals. The patients who would be hooked up to the heart monitor would be considered end users of the heart monitor product. (An end user is the ultimate consumer of the product.)

Most projects are done for internal customers who then represent the needs of customers and end users outside the organization. However, some projects are done directly for an external customer. In these cases, the customer usually pays for the final deliverable directly. An example would be a project in a consulting firm to develop a customized piece of software for an external customer. The external customer would pay based on time and materials or as a flat fee for the project.

Whether the customer is internal or external, there are certain similarities in the role they must play within the project:

✔ Provide the project team with a clear picture of their needs and requirements

✔ Review and approve the charter

✔ Participate on the project team where appropriate

✔ Inform the project leader of any changes in the environment that would affect the project deliverables

✔ Approve changes to the project when needed to make the project a success

✔ Review project status reports

✔ Provide feedback to the project leader on a regular basis

✔ Evaluate the final deliverables as well as the project process

There are some additional roles that internal customers typically perform:

✔ Review and approve the entire project plan (External customers usually review only the scope section of the plan)

✔ Review the final status report

If you have a project with an external customer, it is imperative to have an internal sponsor working on the project. The internal sponsor's job is to balance the needs of the external customer with the needs of the internal organization. If your project has an internal customer, the internal customer may double as the project sponsor.

RESOURCE OR FUNCTIONAL MANAGER ROLE

The resource or functional manager is usually the overseer of the resources (primarily people) that you'll need to do the project. The people who work on the project report to the resource manager and they are then assigned to the project on either a full or, more often, a part-time basis. It is a challenge of the project leader to gain the cooperation and commitment of these people who do not report to him or her. That challenge is met most easily by using a participative project management approach.

The role of the resource manager is to

✔ Provide people to be project team members.

✔ Review and approve the project plan for their areas.

✔ Provide direction, as required, to the team member who represents the resource department.

✔ Make sure the people working on the project from the department have the appropriate level of skill and expertise to do the work.

✔ Make sure team members are provided with the time to complete the project, as defined in the approved project plan.

✔ Remove obstacles for the project team.

A project runs smoothly if everyone performs his or her role. Nevertheless, it is primarily the job of the project leader, with the help of the sponsor, to ensure these roles are fulfilled. Roles vary depending on the phase that the project is in. Let's examine the four phases, or major subdivisions, within the project management process.

THE FOUR PHASES OF A PROJECT

The sequence of activities that each team must complete, from commissioning the project through its completion, is essentially the same for every project, whether the project is simple or complex, large or small, involves a few people or many people. These activities can be grouped into four project phases. A phase of a project constitutes a major set of activities that must be performed within the project management process. These four phases are done in sequence, starting with initiation and ending with close out.

Initiation

The first phase, initiation, begins after the project is selected to be a project by the management team. The purpose of the initiation phase is to provide direction to the project team about what should be accomplished and what constraints exist. The output of the first phase is a document called a charter. The initiation phase is the responsibility of the sponsor, but in most organizations, the project leader actually writes the charter document and then has the sponsor approve it. (See Table 1.2.)

Planning

The next project management phase is called planning. (See Table 1.3.) During planning, the project team develops a plan for how and when the

TABLE 1.2 Initiation Phase		
Phase	*Task Description*	*Output*
Initiation	✔ Broad direction for the project is provided to the project leader by the sponsor. Limits, constraints, and project priorities are defined.	Charter

21

TABLE 1.3 Planning Phase		
Phase	*Task Description*	*Output*
Planning	✔ Select the team members	Project Plan
	✔ Define the scope of the project	
	✔ Define any risks associated with the project and develop ways to prevent them	
	✔ Determine the resources required to complete the project	

work will be accomplished. Planning is the most critical phase of a project, because it is in planning that decisions are made about who will do what and how to ensure everyone works together. If you skip the planning stage and let the team go off to do what they think needs to get done, the important pieces of the project puzzle will be missed. As a result, you'll end up with rework, which is expensive, time consuming, and frustrating. When you plan the work upfront so everyone understands the overall project and is on the same page, the project will go much more smoothly.

The output of the planning phase is a project plan document, which a complete plan for how the project will be executed. The sponsor, customer, and resource managers approve this document.

Execution

After the project plan is approved, the plan is then executed. During the execution phase, the work of the project—creating the deliverables—is done. To make sure the work is on track, the team monitors project progress, and if required, recommends changes to the project plan. The team also communicates project progress to stakeholders. At the end of the execution phase, the final deliverable is delivered to the project customer. (See Table 1.4.)

TABLE 1.4 Execution Phase		
Phase	*Task Description*	*Output*
Execution	✔ Create the deliverables	Status reports
	✔ Monitor project progress	Final deliverable
	✔ Resolve issues	
	✔ Communicate progress	
	✔ Manage changes to the plan	

Close Out

After the customer accepts the final deliverable, the close-out phase begins. In this phase the customer evaluates his or her satisfaction with the project. The sponsor and the team also do project evaluations. Then the team discusses what it learned from the project and translates these lessons into recommendations for improving the organization's overall project management system. A final status report on the project is issued and included in the final project report, also known as the close-out report. This report is sent to the sponsor, customer, and key stakeholders. (See Table 1.5.)

When the close-out report is complete, the project is over. But, it's important to remember to celebrate, not only at the end of the close-out phase, but throughout the project, whenever the team has accomplished something important.

The project's phases can also be seen as a process flow chart as shown in Figure 1.4.

TABLE 1.5 Close-Out Phase		
Phase	*Task Description*	*Output*
Close out	✔ Evaluation of customer satisfaction	Close-out report
	✔ Assessment of lessons learned	

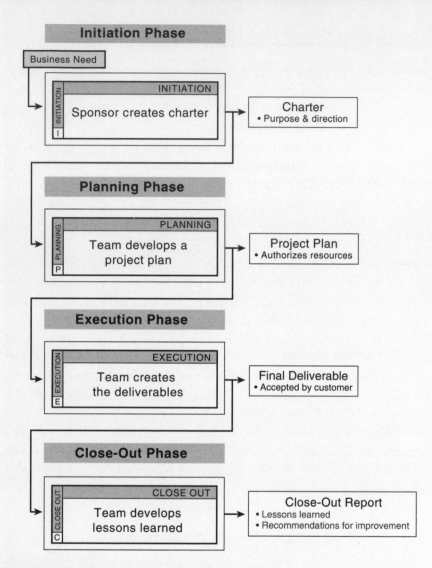

Figure 1.4 Process flow chart of project phases.

PROGRESSION OF PHASES

Each phase builds on the phases that preceded it. If you do a poor job during initiation, then the next three phases will suffer. If you do a bad job of planning, execution and close out will suffer. If you do a bad job of execution, the entire project suffers.

Each phase ends with an approval process that must be completed before moving on to the next phase. This keeps you from skipping ahead to the next phase prematurely. The approvals at the end of a phase are called phase gates. (See Table 1.6.)

One of the benefits of having approvals at the end of each phase is that it minimizes the cost of the project, because project expenditure increases exponentially as you move from initiation to planning to execution. The costs then drop off dramatically during close out. By making sure you've covered all your bases before you move to the next phase, you'll not only minimize costs, but avoid wasting time as well. (See Figure 1.5.)

Whenever you are spending significant resources, be that in actual money or in the form of people's time, it's helpful to have go/no-go decision gates, such as phase gates, that force a decision to continue with the project. If you have a medium or long project (over six months duration) you'll also want to include some go/no-go decision gates throughout the execution phase to make sure there is agreement that you're doing the right things and that the deliverables you are producing are still needed by

TABLE 1.6 Phase Gates	
Phase	*Phase Gate*
Initiation	Approved charter
Planning	Approved project plan
Execution	Accepted final deliverable
Close out	Approved close-out report

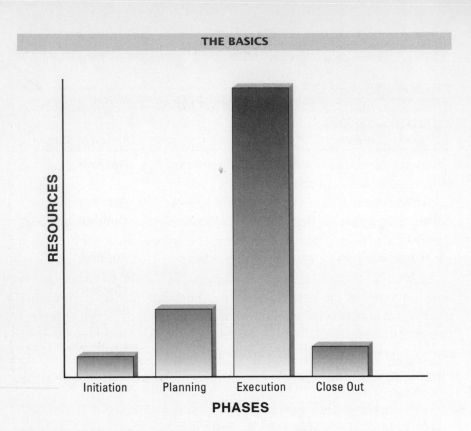

Figure 1.5 Illustration of expenditures vs. phases.

the customer and the organization. These execution go/no-go decision points are called stage gates and they should be set by the sponsor.

APPROVALS IN THE PROJECT MANAGEMENT PROCESS

The approvals for moving from one phase to another, or to pass through a stage gate should be part of the organization's project management system, which is set up and maintained by management. Suggestions for approvals in the project management process are as follows (Table 1.7):

TABLE 1.7 Gate Approvals			
Project Management Process Component	Sponsor	Customer*	Resource Manager
Charter	Write and Approve	Approve	Approve
Project Plan	Approve	Approve	Approve
Execution Stage Gates	Approve	Approve	Optional approval
Change Requests	Approve	Approve	Approve if area is affected
Close-Out Report	Approve	Receive	Receive

*When you have an external customer, you'll need to determine which documents are appropriate for him or her to review and approve.

PROJECT SUCCESS

A project is successful when the needs of both the customer and the organization have been satisfied and when there has been organizational learning as a result of the project. Customers are satisfied when you provide a deliverable(s) that meets their needs and exceeds their expectations. The deliverable can be a product (something tangible or intangible), a service, a process, a plan, or a combination of these.

Customers are delighted when the final deliverable exceeds their expectations. They are disappointed when their expectations are not met. (See Table 1.8.)

Expectations can be managed. A good rule is to underpromise what you plan to deliver. If customers expect less than what they end up getting, they are delighted. But if they expect more than they get, they will be disappointed. In both cases you have delivered the same deliverable; the only difference is what is in the mind of the customers about what they will be receiving—their expectations.

27

TABLE 1.8 Customer Expectations	
Customer Response	*Deliverable vs. Expectations*
Delighted	Final deliverable exceeds expectations
Satisfied	Final deliverable meets expectations
Dissatisfied	Final deliverable falls short of expectations

The second measure of project success is that you have satisfied the needs of the organization. These needs may be such things as making a profit or developing capability in a new area of technology. The needs of the organization are represented by the sponsor and should be included in the charter.

The third measure of project success is that you, the team, and the organization learn something as a result of the project, so that next time, you or someone else in the organization can build on your successes and avoid your mistakes. This learning process should go on throughout the project and is the primary purpose of the close-out phase.

Now that we've covered the basics, it's time to march on down the road to explore the first project phase, initiation, in more depth.

Initiating a Project

The first phase of a project, which is called initiation, begins after management decides to authorize the project. The goal of initiation is to set the direction for your project—what the project is expected to accomplish—and define any constraints on the project. Both project direction and constraints should come from the sponsor, because the sponsor is the management person who is accountable for ensuring that the project meets the strategic goals of the organization and that the benefits of the project outweigh its costs.

The direction and constraints for the project are outlined in a document called the charter. This document is the responsibility of the sponsor. However, many sponsors either don't know how to write a charter or claim not to have the time to do so. As a result, it's very probable that you'll find yourself writing the charter for the sponsor and then have the sponsor review and approve it when you're done. (In addition, you'll want the project customer to approve the charter, if possible.)

The charter should answer these basic questions about the project: What are you supposed to produce? For whom? By when? And for how much money?

We will be designing and installing a fulfillment operation in the XYZ Company as our example for completing a charter. (Currently XYZ's fulfillment process, picking orders, packing, shipping, receiving inventory, has been done by an outside contractor. The management team has decided that this process needs to be brought inside the company. The manager who will be accountable for the fulfillment business process when it is installed, Ken, is the project sponsor.)

It is easier to complete a charter if you use a form or template. (The forms shown in this book can be purchased from the author's web site at www.projectresults.com.) Let's walk through each section of completing a generic charter form.

WRITING THE SCOPE SECTION

The first section of a charter is called the scope section and it defines what will be produced for whom.

The first entry in the scope section form is the project name. Keep the name short and easy to say because you'll be writing and saying it over and over again. The name should reflect the main purpose of the project.(See Table 2.1.)

Next, describe the business case for the project. What are the business needs that justify the project? How does this project help to support the strategic objectives of the organization? How will it improve the organization? What benefits will the organization realize as a result of doing this project? (See Table 2.2.)

Under project objectives, describe the purpose of the project. This should be a brief statement or a couple of bullet points about what the project will accomplish.

Make sure that the statement of purpose only includes things that you're willing to be accountable for. Any benefits that the organization will receive as a result of doing the project should be included in the

TABLE 2.1 Generic Charter Form—Scope Section	
Topic	*Description*
Project Name	Name of the project. It should reflect the main objectives of the project.

TABLE 2.2 Generic Charter Form—Scope Section	
Topic	Description
Business Case	The business reasons for the project. This section explains why the project is important to the organization.

business case and not in the objectives. The sponsor is accountable to make sure the project meets the needs of the organization. The project leader is accountable to make sure the project meets the project objectives. Organizational benefits of a project are outside the scope of the project and should not be included as objectives. (See Table 2.3.)

For example, one of the reasons for bringing the XYZ fulfillment process inside is to save the organization money over the long term. This is a business reason for the project. Therefore, it should not be included as a project objective because the project team, which will disband after the close-out phase, cannot be held accountable for long-term results. In addition, the appropriate person in the organization to be held accountable for long-term savings for the fulfillment process would be Ken, the process manager, not the project team. An appropriate project objective would be to install a cost-effective fulfillment process that begins at order entry and ends at payment.

Next, define the final deliverable of the project. A final deliverable can be a product, service, process, plan, or a combination of the above. The final deliverable is the final output from the execution phase of the project that is delivered to the project customer. It is also the primary reason the project has been undertaken, because projects exist to satisfy

TABLE 2.3 Generic Charter Form—Scope Section	
Topic	Description
Project Objectives	Purpose of the project. The project team will be held accountable for achieving the project objectives.

a customer, and customer satisfaction is achieved when the final deliverable meets or exceeds the customer's expectations (See Table 2.4.).

If there is more than one final deliverable, define each one. For example, if you're producing a product, you may need to design the process that will create it. Or, if you're producing a service, you may need a supporting product, like workshop materials if the service is a training program. Beware of a charter that contains many final deliverables. It may be a sign that the scope is too broad. Try to keep the number of deliverables to one or two. This will help to keep the scope of the project to a manageable size. (See Table 2.5.)

The project customer is the person or group who receives the final deliverable. If you're designing and implementing a business process, then your project customer should be the business process manager who will run the business process when you're done. If you're developing a product or service, then your customer may be whoever has to

TABLE 2.4 Generic Charter Form—Scope Section	
Topic	Description
Final Deliverable(s)	The end product, service, process, or plan that will be created for the project customer.

TABLE 2.5 Types of Final Deliverables	
Final Deliverable Type	Description
Product	A tangible or intangible good
Process	A set of steps that produces a product
Service	The act of one person doing for another
	A service is supported by a process, but the service itself is created at the moment it is delivered, like teaching
Plan	A document that describes how something will be or should be accomplished

sell that product or service. Ask yourself, "Who will I hand off the final deliverable to?" This is your project customer. (See Table 2.6.)

Beware of confusing the project customer with the end user, the person or group that will ultimately consume what you are producing. The project customer is the person or group that actually receives the project's final deliverable. Still confused? Don't worry. We'll talk more about project customers in Chapter 5.

Next, document the characteristics that the customer is looking for from the final deliverable. What does he or she require from the final deliverable in terms of performance (functions) or in terms of features (bells and whistles)? These are the customer's requirements, and at this stage they will be broadly defined. You shouldn't list more than half a dozen key functions and features because you generally don't know a lot yet. You'll come back and expand these during project planning. For now, you just need to get an overview of what the customer is looking for, from his or her point of view. The best way to get this list of requirements is to ask the customer directly. (See Table 2.7.)

The last section in the scope section of the charter is customer need. This is the problem the customer is trying to solve by means of the final deliverable. Customers don't really need deliverables. What they need is a solution to a problem. For example, you don't really need

TABLE 2.6 Generic Charter Form—Scope Section	
Topic	*Description*
Project Customer	The group(s) that receives the final deliverables from the project

TABLE 2.7 Generic Charter Form—Scope Section	
Topic	*Description*
Customer Requirements	Specific features or functions of the final deliverable

a car. What you need is a means of transportation and/or a status symbol. The car is a means of satisfying your need.

In the customer-needs section you're trying to define the real reason the project is being undertaken for the customer: the problem they have that will be relieved through the production of your final deliverable. (The problem will not necessarily disappear after your project is completed, but it should be alleviated through the use of your final deliverable.) For our fulfillment process, the customer is the fulfillment business process manager (Ken) and the need or problem is that shipping of training materials through an outside vendor is unreliable and inaccurate. By knowing the need, you can continually check to see that what you are doing will help to satisfy the customer need. If the answer is no, you know you're going in the wrong direction. Knowing the need is one of the compasses you'll use to keep your project on track. (See Table 2.8.)

Sit down with the customer and ask the customer what the business problem is that he or she expects the final deliverable to help resolve. The better you understand the need that is driving the project, the more likely you'll be to satisfy the customer at the end.

Finally, list the project's stakeholders. (See Table 2.9.) Stake-

TABLE 2.8 Generic Charter Form—Scope Section	
Topic	Description
Customer Needs	The customer problem that the final deliverable will help to solve

TABLE 2.9 Generic Charter Form—Scope Section	
Topic	Description
Stakeholders	Anyone who will be affected by the project, other than the project customer, sponsor, or team members

holders are people or groups who will be affected by the project. These can include major suppliers, resource managers, or any groups that might be affected by the deliverable of the project, like a worker's union, for example. Customers, the sponsor, and team members are also stakeholders, but they will be identified in other sections of the charter document.

THE SCOPE SECTION FOR THE FULFILLMENT PROJECT

This completes the scope section, which should broadly address the questions why, and what.(See Table 2.10.) Now it's time to define the constraints that the project must operate within. This is detailed in the resources section.

WRITING THE RESOURCES SECTION

The second section, called Resources, relates to who, when, and how much. The first question, who, refers to who will be on the project team.

If you're writing the charter, now is a good time to take your first pass at determining who should be on your team. (See Table 2.11.) Review the scope section of the charter. What skills will you need to create the final deliverable required by the customer? Which stakeholders do you want as members of the team? (See the Assembling the Team section at the end of this chapter for more information.) If the sponsor is writing the charter, then the sponsor has the option of appointing members of the team or just appointing the project leader and letting the project leader choose the team.

Next, define the limits for the project. First, what is the deadline for the final deliverable? If there are no deadlines, are there expectations about when the final deliverable will be completed? If not, indicate that there is no deadline. (This is rare. Usually there is a deadline

TABLE 2.10   Scope Section of Charter for Fulfillment Project

Topic	Description
Project Name	Order/fulfillment
Business Case	The business is projecting a continued 25% growth rate per year. An assessment of the core competencies required to sustain this growth concludes that we need to bring our fulfillment service in house. This will reduce our overall costs, but more importantly, it will increase customer satisfaction.
Project Objectives	Design and install a cost-effective fulfillment process that begins at order entry and ends at payment
Final Deliverable(s)	Order/fulfillment process installed
Project Customers	Business process owner—Ken
Customer Requirements	1. A fulfillment process that will handle order variation by customer 2. Integration with the accounting system 3. Inventory tracking ability 4. Order accuracy
Customer Needs	Training-material orders vary by program and by customer; thus unlike book fulfillment, there is considerable variation between orders. Outside contractors have proved unable to deal with the variation and the short lead times associated with our business. Currently customer satisfaction is maintained through extraordinary effort by internal staff.
Stakeholders	Accounting, sales

TABLE 2.11   Generic Charter Form—Resources Section

Topic	Description
Team Assignments	People assigned to the project team

and often it is unrealistic.) Are there any other deadlines that the team must meet? Include an explanation of why each deadline has been set. This will help the team understand the reasons for the deadlines.

The deadline section should not be used to create a schedule for the team. That's micromanagement and it is neither helpful to the team, nor will it improve the team's chances of completing the project on time. During the planning process, the team will create a schedule they can live with, and the sponsor and customer will then have an opportunity to review and approve it. (See Table 2.12.)

Is there a limit on the amount of time that people can spend on the project? The time that internal people spend on a project is called staff-effort time or just staff effort. Sometimes organizations decide that people should not spend more than X percent of their time on a project or that the project should not require more than Y total person hours. If you have a staff-effort limit of any sort, list it here. Also, list the reasons for the limit. (See Table 2.13.)

What about money? What's the maximum amount of money that can be spent on this project? Try to find out how much money has been allocated to the project, even if you don't have a project budget. In many organizations, the managers of the resource areas spend the

TABLE 2.12 Generic Charter Form—Resources Section	
Topic	Description
Deadlines	Dates for delivery of the final deliverable(s); reasons for the deadline

TABLE 2.13 Generic Charter Form—Resources Section	
Topic	Description
Staff-Effort Limit	Maximum amount of internal effort authorized for the project; reasons for the limit

money, not the project manager. If this is the case, list the amount of money available from each department for the project. This will be important in trying to plan your project spending during the planning phase. List any reasons for setting the spending limit at the amount designated. (See Table 2.14.)

Are there any other constraints on your resources? Anything you cannot do? An example of a constraint would be not hiring consultants or only using existing equipment. List any constraints the sponsor has placed on the project (Table 2.15).

Finally, the team needs to know the priorities within the project (Table 2.16). What is most important: scope, schedule, or cost? These three variables are interdependent and it's important to know their order

TABLE 2.14 Generic Charter Form—Resources Section	
Topic	Description
Spending Limit	Maximum amount of money authorized for the project; reasons for the limit

TABLE 2.15 Generic Charter Form—Resources Section	
Topic	Description
Organizational Constraints	Constraints, other than deadlines, staff effort, and spending, which the project must live within

TABLE 2.16 Generic Charter Form—Resources Section	
Topic	Description
Project Priorities	The ranking of scope, schedule, and cost

of importance because, during the planning phase you'll have to make trade-off decisions between them.

They are known as the triple constraint. (See Figure 2.1.) Expanding or contracting one of these items affects the other two. For example, if we add more functions to our fulfillment center, like having the capability of automated picking, then we'll need to lengthen our timeline and increase our budget. Shortening the schedule can usually be done by either adding more effort and/or money, or by reducing the scope.

In order for the team to make the best choices between the three variables, they need to know how the sponsor prioritizes scope versus schedule versus cost. Is schedule the most important with scope next and then the cost? Or, is scope first (make sure the customer is delighted) and then cost and finally schedule. One way to ascertain the priorities is to ask the sponsor, "If you had your choice of exceeding customer expectations, bringing the project in early or coming in under budget, which would be your first choice? Second? Last?"

Number the variables from one to three with one being the highest priority. If one variable is much more important than the other two, put an asterisk next to it. Explain the reasons for the way the priorities were set. In our example below, the priorities are schedule, scope, and

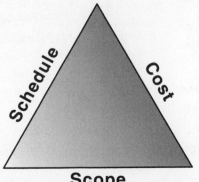

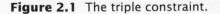

Figure 2.1 The triple constraint.

then cost. That means completing the project early is the highest priority. Adding to the scope is second, and reducing cost is third.

THE RESOURCES SECTION OF OUR SAMPLE PROJECT

Let's take a look at the resources section of our project charter for our fulfillment project. (See Table 2.17.)

The charter sets the stage for the rest of the project and it is the first pass at defining exactly what will be required for the project. For these reasons, it is probably one of the most difficult tasks in the project management process. If you have to write the charter for the sponsor, ask him or her to give you their input and get inputs from the project customer as well.

TABLE 2.17 Resources Section of Charter for Fulfillment Project	
Topic	*Description*
Team Assignments	Carolyn, project leader
Deadline	December 31
Staff Effort Limit	Maximum of 25% of total effort by project team members and 50% of the project leader's total effort. (Team members must be able to maintain their regular job responsibilities.)
Spending Limit	$25,000
Organizational Constraints	Use existing computer hardware
Project Priorities	1. Schedule (contract on outside fulfillment service expires on 12/31)
	2. Scope
	3. Cost

GETTING THE CHARTER APPROVED

Review the draft of the charter with your sponsor. Review the scope section with the customer to make sure he or she agrees with your definition of what will be produced by the project. Also, review the deadline date with the customer, and if the customer is paying for the project, review the staff-effort and spending limits as well. Ask the customer to sign the charter.

If the customer requests changes to the charter, review these with the sponsor. When you and the sponsor are comfortable with the document, you should both sign it. Where appropriate, ask the customer to sign it as well.

The approval of the charter launches the next phase of the project, which is planning, setting the stage for how planning will be done. Too many times, teams rush off and begin planning, only to find out that they have invested days or even weeks planning the wrong thing. Don't let that happen to you. Take a little extra time up front to get the charter right and you'll save yourself a lot of time and aggravation later on.

Before you begin planning, you'll need to set up your issues and lessons-learned lists.

THE ISSUES LIST

The first planning tool you'll want to create is the issues list. This list will capture any issues that need resolution or any actions that need to be completed that cannot be captured in the project schedule, which you'll develop later during the planning phase. (From now on we'll refer to both issues and actions as issues.) The issues list is set up and managed by the project leader. (See Figure 2.2.)

The first column is the issue number. Each issue should be given a unique, consecutive number. If you use a spreadsheet program to track your issues, you can have it number the issues for you.

ISSUES LIST							
Project Name:			Project Sponsor:				
Issue #	Description of issue	Person who needs resolution	Person responsible to resolve	Date resolution needed	Date resolved	How resolved?	
1							
2							
3							
4							
5							

Figure 2.2 Issues list.

In the next column write a brief description of the issue or action item required. What exactly must be resolved?

Next, who is it that needs the issue resolved? Whose problem is it? Then record the name of the person on the team who is accountable to resolve the issue. He or she may or may not resolve the issue alone, but he or she needs to get the issue resolved. (Because we can hold only members of the team accountable, the person whose job it is to get the issue resolved must be on the team.) Next, when is the resolution needed? Set a date.

The last two columns are filled in after the issue has been resolved.

THE PROPER USE OF AN ISSUES LIST

The issues list is maintained by the project leader and is updated at each project team meeting. It is not a replacement for a project schedule. It is used during the planning phase, before a schedule is created, to track any planning tasks that must be completed. It is also used during execution to track issues or action items that are not significant enough to put on the schedule. It should not be used to track the deliverables or tasks that must be completed during the execution phase—the real work of creating the final deliverable. That is what the schedule is for.

MONITORING THE ISSUES LIST

The issues list should be monitored and updated at every team meeting. Review the current issues with the team, asking for a status update on the issues due for resolution. Were they resolved? If so, how? When? If they were not resolved, what will be required to get them resolved and when will that happen? Ideally, the project leader should be notified as soon as the person assigned to the issue knows that he will not be able to resolve the issue or when he needs help getting the issue resolved on time. This allows the project leader to be proactive before the issue is overdue. If necessary, enlist the help of the sponsor, if the project team can't get an issue resolved on its own.

Before the project team meeting is adjourned, review any items that should be resolved before the next team meeting, so that everyone is clear about which pending issues are scheduled for resolution.

LESSONS-LEARNED LIST

In addition to an issues list, you'll want to create a lessons-learned list to help you capture what is learned over the course of the project. These lessons will be reviewed and summarized during the close-out phase, but keeping an ongoing list throughout the project will help to prevent losing important lessons that occur through the project process.

A sample lessons-learned list is shown in Figure 2.3.

LESSONS-LEARNED LIST			
Project Name:		Project Leader:	
Lesson #	Description of Incident	Date of Incident	Description of Lessons Learned
1			
2			
3			
4			

Figure 2.3 Lessons-learned list.

ASSEMBLING THE PROJECT TEAM

You've got a charter and you've set up your issues and lessons-learned lists; now it's time to gather together your initial project team. It's called the initial team because, until you're done planning, you can't be entirely sure what team members you'll need in order to execute the project. You'll pull together an initial team now, to work through the planning phase and hopefully it will be the same team you'll need for execution. Take some time up front to consider whom you'll need on the team, because it's best not to have to switch team members midstream.

Even if your sponsor assigns you an initial team, do the following analysis to see if there are any major holes that you should fill before moving on to planning.

The first thing you'll need to assess is whether you have a large or a small project, because the composition of the team depends on the size of the project. (See Table 2.18.)

SMALL PROJECTS

Small projects are ones that require ten or fewer people to do the project work. In other words, they can be managed with a relatively small group of people and, therefore, all of the people doing the

TABLE 2.18 Large vs. Small Projects	
Project Size	Description
Small Project	Ten or fewer team members required to complete the project's tasks
Large Project	More than ten team members required to complete the project

work can be part of the main project team. For small projects, the first priority for selecting team members will be their skills, knowledge, and experience relevant to the work that must be done on the project.

To determine the best team composition, make a list of the major resource areas you'll be using to create the final deliverable for the project. Then approach each resource manager and ask him or her to help you assess the types of skills you'll need to get the project done. The resource manager can then match the skills required to the people available. In contrast, asking for someone by name can cause resistance. You'll usually get more cooperation from the resource manager by specifying the types of skills that you require.

The next thing you'll need to do is review the stakeholder list from the charter and see if you've got each major stakeholder area adequately represented on the team. Stakeholders are affected by the project and anyone or any group that will be significantly affected by the project is going to want a voice in how the project is done. It's best to get these people involved right from the start because

- ✔ You can incorporate their concerns and ideas into the project process.
- ✔ They can make a contribution to the outcome of the project.
- ✔ By participating in the project, they'll understand the decisions that are made and buy into those decisions.
- ✔ They will be project supporters instead of detractors.

It's particularly important to include them on the team if you're doing a project that involves implementation. Many implementation projects fail because the people who will be affected by the implementation block any progress. In our fulfillment example, we would want Ken, the business-process manager, on the team because it will be his job to run the fulfillment center after we've got it designed and installed.

LARGE PROJECTS

If you're working on a large project, one that has more than ten team members, then you'll need to divide the main project into subprojects. A subproject is a subsection of the main project. In a large project, each subproject consists of a team of people, overseen by a subproject leader. The subproject leader performs the same role as the project leader, except that he or she leads the subproject team instead of the main project. (See Figure 2.4.)

The reason for breaking the main project down into subprojects is that when you have more than ten people on a team, the group is too large to collaborate effectively. It's better to break the group into subgroups or subprojects so each team is a manageable size. In large projects, the main project team will consist of subproject leaders. They will

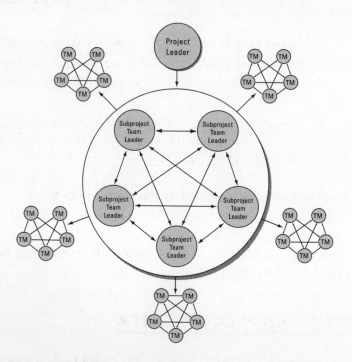

Figure 2.4 Large project with subprojects.

each have a subproject team (if they need help getting the work done) composed of people who actually do the work (TM), create the deliverables, of the subproject. These subproject deliverables must all come together to create the final deliverable for the main project. One of the jobs of the subproject leaders is to make sure all the deliverables for the subproject meet the needs of the main project.

Therefore, in a large project, the main project team is composed of the subproject team leaders who are usually representatives from the key stakeholder groups (usually from each of the resource functions). Review your stakeholder areas to identify which ones you'll need to include on your team.

Follow these guidelines for choosing subproject leaders:

- ✔ You'll need the same skills for subproject leaders as for the project leader. Subproject leaders are often project leaders in training.
- ✔ They should be able to make decisions for their resource area.
- ✔ They should be a good ambassador for the stakeholder area— representing the stakeholder interests but also balancing those with the project interests.
- ✔ They should be good at selling the project to the stakeholder group. It's their job to get the stakeholder group to buy into the decisions made by the project team.

The deliverables get created at the subproject level, so this is where the work skills will be needed. The subproject leaders can do the skill assessments for their teams.

Once the initial team has been assembled, it's time to get them together and kick off the project.

CONTENT AND PROCESS CHECK

Before moving onto the project kick off, it's useful to do a content and process check to make sure you haven't missed anything.

❑ Did you or your sponsor draft the charter, completely documenting the expectations and constraints for the project?

❑ Did you get inputs from the customer on the scope section of the charter?

❑ Did you get the sponsor and customer to sign the charter when it was completed?

❑ Did you set up your issues list?

❑ Did you set up a lessons-learned list?

❑ Have you assembled an initial team that will do an effective job of creating the plan for the project?

Chapter 3

Leading the Project Team

It's important to remember that the project leader does not complete a project alone. Most projects require a diversity of skills, experience, and specialized expertise in order to create the deliverable for the customer. That means a group of people will be needed, with each person contributing something unique, and each one depending on the others to get his or her job done. By developing group members into a team you manage the interdependence in such a group. Through the interactions within the team, the raw materials of information, ideas, and knowledge are synthesized and then transformed into deliverables that will meet the project's objectives.

A team is created when people work together, functioning as if they were a single unit. Seven principles of creating a team can help guide you through this process.

PRINCIPLE 1

People own what they participate in creating. When we invest our time, energy, and ourselves into a process, it becomes ours. We take

49

ownership for it. We accept accountability for it. As Meg Wheatley pointed out in *Leadership and the New Science: Discovering Order in a Chaotic World* (Berrett-Koehler Publishers, 2001), "A tried and true maxim of my field of organizational behavior is that 'people support what they create.'"

The sense of ownership brings with it the feeling of self-determination. This is very different from the feelings that arise when you are at the behest of someone else. Self-determination is motivating; being on the receiving end of delegation is not.

When people on a team work together to create a project plan and monitor and control the project, they take ownership not only for their own work but for the entire project. This ownership takes the monkey off the back of the project leader and allows the leader to share it with the team members. When the team owns the project, they have a sense that they are all in it together. They sink or swim together. This is fundamental to building a real team.

PRINCIPLE 2

Team members who understand the project are more committed to making the project successful. To understand is to make sense of what is required of you and how what you do fits into the whole. Understanding involves taking in of information and knowledge so that it becomes your own.

When people on a team understand the project—why it's being done, what they are supposed to do, how what they do affects others and fits into the whole picture—they are more effective as individuals and more effective as a team. They are also more motivated, because through understanding they engage not only the mind but the heart as well.

Conversely, if an individual only understands his or her own piece of the project, that individual does what is best for him or her, and not necessarily what is best for the project as a whole. This can create inadvertent problems for other team members. For example, let's say you're a part of a project to celebrate the launch of a highly successful new product for your company. You're in charge of food and you decide that it would be easiest to bring in prepackaged meals. However, the clean up subproject is not aware that prepackaged foods would be provided instead of a buffet. As a result, they don't have enough garbage cans to handle the litter. Not a pretty sight.

When everyone understands the whole project, misunderstandings among team members are minimized. Understanding can best be achieved through team participation in the project management process, which creates ownership, understanding, and helps to build the team. Team participation is not the same as team building. Team building is an activity (or activities) that is directed at getting people to better understand and trust each other. It typically has very little to do with understanding the work that must be accomplished. As a result, when people return to doing the work after the team building is over, the same work conflicts erupt again. Don't make the mistake of opting for team building instead of participation. If you exclude the team from the project management activities in the project, you won't be able to develop an effective team, and team-member understanding and ownership will be greatly diminished. What really counts is not artificial team building, but involving the team in the real decision making for the project.

If team participation is so effective, why don't more people do it? First, they claim that they don't have the time for participation. They claim it's faster and easier if the project manager just decides what needs to be done and then delegates tasks to the people on the team. Participation does require more time during the planning phase, but planning is neither the longest phase nor the phase that consumes the most resources. That phase is execution, and lack of team participation during planning adds even more time to the execution phase.

The other objection to team participation is that the project leader will lose control of the project. The leader fears that the team will make bad decisions and he or she will be held accountable for the results. It's true that the leader will be held accountable for the results; however, the path to achieving the best results is through team participation. It has been demonstrated time and time again that groups of people will make better overall decisions than a single decision maker. Most projects are too complex for the project leader to understand everything that goes on in every technical area involved in the project. Also, it's a waste of time and resources for the leader to try to understand everything when he or she has people with the expertise on the team. Why not use them by allowing them to participate?

Project leaders fear losing control, but control merely shifts from the content to the process. The project leader controls the project management process that the team will follow. He or she provides the team with the tools and techniques to help them make good decisions. In this way, the project leader ensures that good outcomes are achieved. The illusion that you have control when you do something yourself is very strong, but being the sole decision maker or planner for the project doesn't usually produce the best results for the project. It is faster and more accurate to engage the team members in helping to create the project plan than trying to do it yourself and sell your plan to team members when you're done. Inevitably, a plan created in a vacuum, by the project leader, is flawed. You're better off relinquishing control of the planning and monitoring decisions and, instead, make sure you have a good process for people to follow so they'll make the right decisions. You can always reserve some decisions for yourself. It's your prerogative as the project leader. Just consider doing it when it will be most effective for the project and for the team.

PRINCIPLE 3

People are inspired by what is meaningful to them. We have a basic desire to create meaning in our lives. We want to engage in activities that fulfill that need for meaning. Projects need to be meaningful to the people who work on them.

To make a project meaningful to the team, you need to connect the project to the strategic goals of the organization. They need to know that management supports the project and that the results of the project are important to the organization.

People want to know that what they will be doing individually is important to the project as a whole. In spite of the fact that people will get paid whether or not the work is important, they don't want to waste their time on busy work. They want to do work that makes a difference.

You can create meaning for people by having them participate in the project management process: by defining the deliverables, assigning accountability, identifying the interdependence of deliverables, and so on. As people understand more about the project, it will become more meaningful to them, assuming the project is needed by the organization. If the project isn't needed, you're in trouble, because very few people are motivated to work on something that will not eventually make a difference. If you're straddled with someone's pet project that no one really cares about and won't help to improve the business, you're fighting a losing battle to build a team. Without meaning, most people are not motivated.

PRINCIPLE 4

Use team-based tools for planning, monitoring, idea generation, decision making, and conflict resolution so that the team can make good decisions and reach consensus quickly.

Team-based tools allow the entire team to participate in the process at hand, whether that involves planning, decision making, idea generation, or conflict resolution. They provide a structured way for everyone on the team to contribute and make decisions by consensus. Consensus does not mean that each person gets his or her first choice. What it does mean is that everyone agrees that they can live with the decision that has been made. It doesn't mean that everyone necessarily agrees with the decision.

You can tell if you have consensus by simply asking. Go around the room and ask each person if he can live with the decision that has been reached. If someone says, no, then ask that person what would be required in order for the decision to be acceptable. See if a compromise can be reached that everyone can agree to. Sometimes you can't reach consensus. Sometimes you'll need to make the call and dictate the decision. It's best to reserve this option when consensus is not possible.

Using team-based tools will help the group reach consensus with minimal conflicts. The tools you'll be learning for managing projects are team-based tools. They

✔ Encourage participation by team members.

✔ Encourage everyone to contribute.

✔ Are structured so that there is a systematic way of working through the steps of the tool.

✔ Lead to consensus.

Team-based tools should incorporate all three sensory learning styles—visual, auditory, and kinesthetic. Sensory learning styles are the ways in which individuals take in and process information.

Visual learners need to see what is going on. They take in information through visual means—written documents, flip charts, overheads. Team-based tools should make visible everyone's inputs, ideas, and comments. This is typically done by working with self-stick notes on flip-chart or banner paper taped to the wall. In this way everyone sees the same set of information.

Auditory learners learn by hearing and talking. They need to be involved in a discussion in order to fully comprehend the issue at hand. When a decision is reached, it is important to restate the decision verbally and ask for verbal agreement from team members. Team-based tools should include a vehicle for discussing the ideas or issues being worked on.

Kinesthetic learners learn best while doing or sensing. They need to get the feel for the ideas or issues and they do this best while physically moving around. Team-based tools should incorporate movement in the exercises, where team members move self-stick notes from one place to another, physically organizing the ideas being worked on.

The team-based project management tools we'll be covering in this book cover all three sensory learning styles. They involve visual information that is recorded on flip-chart and banner paper, discussion, and then physical involvement by team members. By using these tools, you'll ensure that everyone on the team is engaged in the process and is taking in and understanding the information being presented. We'll discuss decision-making tools more extensively in Chapter 11.

PRINCIPLE 5

Show your appreciation for the contributions of each individual on the team and for the team as a whole. When people feel valued, they do a better job. When the team is valued, it performs better. Not everyone on a team will feel valued in the same way. However, there are some standard ways in which to value people and teams:

- ✔ Recognize accomplishments.
- ✔ Thank people for the work they do.
- ✔ Celebrate successes.
- ✔ Respect each person's inputs and opinions.
- ✔ Stand up for the team.
- ✔ Be honest.

You'll need to take time at each team meeting to recognize accomplishments and thank people for their contributions. In addition, when significant accomplishments are achieved, take time for a small celebration. It can be something small like bringing cookies to the meeting or having a pizza party. If possible, build some money into the project budget to allow you to celebrate at least on a small scale.

As important as recognition and celebration are, it's equally important for the team to feel you're on their side, and if they take a risk, you'll support them. You are the shield that stands between them and the outside world, providing them a safe place to work on the project.

PRINCIPLE 6

To build a team you must build and maintain an environment of mutual trust and respect.

Trust takes time to build. Tips for building trust include the following:

✔ Honor diversity of thinking, learning, and other individual differences.

✔ Don't make promises you can't keep.

✔ Keep your commitments.

✔ Maintain confidences.

✔ Value each person's inputs and ideas.

✔ Be honest.

✔ Use good people skills.

✔ Use good facilitation skills.

✔ Eliminate blame.

Although trust is built slowly, it can be destroyed in an instant, and when it has been destroyed, rebuilding trust takes a very long time. Therefore, take the time to develop and maintain trust between you and the team, and between members of the team. If you do something that depletes their trust in you, admit your mistake openly, make amends, and ask for forgiveness. That will help you to rebuild your trust account. If you're open and honest, people will allow you a few blemishes. If you pretend you're perfect, they won't allow you a single error.

PRINCIPLE 7

Empower the team. Empowered teams are more effective than disempowered ones. An empowered team is one in which decision making and responsibility have been pushed down as far as possible. When a team is empowered, they take more accountability for the outcomes they must produce. In addition, empowerment allows the team to share the burden of the project with the project leader. To properly empower a team you need to do the following:

✔ Clearly define the roles that each person involved with the project will play and hold each person to those roles.

✔ Clearly define what is expected from the team and from each individual on it.

✔ Provide adequate resources to get the job done. It is the project leader's job, with the help of the sponsor, to ensure that the team has the resources to complete the project. If, after the team does the planning, there are not sufficient resources to produce the final deliverable, then the project leader must negotiate with the sponsor for more resources or for a change in the scope. There is nothing motivating or empowering about trying to get a job done without adequate time or money to complete the task or without the resources that were promised.

✔ Make sure the people on the team have the skills and knowledge to get the job done. Make sure your team has the project and team skills it will need to be successful.

✔ Clearly define accountability for results. Empowerment carries with it the burden of accountability, to answer for the outcomes that are assigned to you. In our CORE PM™ method, every deliverable, every task, and every issue has assigned accountability. In addition, there is a feedback mechanism so that the leader and the team know how well each person has fulfilled his or her accountability.

✔ Push decision making down to the lowest level possible. You don't want to micromanage the team or the individuals on the team. The main concern at the team level should be on deliverables and issues that affect multiple people on the team. Too many teams get involved in the minutiae of what each individual is doing. By clearly defining accountability and by making sure that people have the skills or the support they need to get the job done, there is no reason to focus on things that are best left to the individual.

Most project managers have been trained to be content driven. They make the decisions. They know what's best. They solve the project's problems. But this focus on content does not produce great project results.

In order to let go of control and empower the team, you'll need to help the team clearly define what needs to be done, who is accountable, when it needs to be completed, and then make sure people have the resources and skills to get the job done. You should require regular reporting from the team on the deliverables or issues assigned. This closes the accountability loop; accountability has been assigned and the person accountable reports back on the fulfillment of that accountability.

These seven basic principles will help you create a more effective team. But teams don't just emerge, fully formed, and performing at peak capacity. They evolve, through stages (see Figure 3.1).

The first four stages were defined by Bruce Tuckman.

THE FORMING STAGE

The first stage is called forming, and it occurs when the team first comes together. When a team is forming, they are focused on answering the following questions.

- ✔ Why are we here?
- ✔ What is my role in this endeavor?
- ✔ Who are these other people and how will we get along?
- ✔ What's the project leader like and how will he or she run this project?

In the forming stage, team members are polite. They are waiting to see what will happen. What you will hear during forming is, "Why?

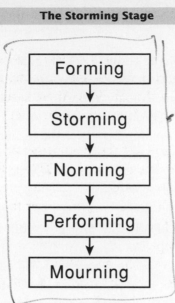

Figure 3.1 Stages of team development.

What? Who? When?" This stage in a project begins at the kick off of the project and it ends when people stop being polite and conflicts begin to emerge.

It's important to manage this stage carefully so that you can move quickly into the next stage: storming. In Chapter 4, we'll discuss how you manage project kick off so that you set the right tone for the project and move through this first stage of team formation quickly.

If you're successful at the forming stage, the team will naturally move on to the next stage of development: storming.

THE STORMING STAGE

Right after the kick-off process, when people are feeling a little more comfortable with each other, and the realization of the actual challenges of the work sets in, the storming stage erupts and destroys the artificial tranquility of the group. Disagreements arise about what needs to be done and who will do it. Groups may divide into opposing factions. Listen for, "I can't," and "That's not possible" to know you're in storming. The greater the stretch goals (goals that are difficult to achieve) for the project, the more vocal the storming stage will be. However, the more management support you have and the more meaningful the purpose of the project, the easier it will be to resolve the conflicts. Having a strong common goal for the project is one of the most important driving forces to resolving conflicts.

As much as you might like to, you can't skip the storming stage. Storming is a necessary and useful stage if you want to create understanding, alignment, and ownership. This is when people merge their individual perceptions of how the project should be done and mold a group perception.

Storming may last through much of the planning process. It's healthy to have conflicts over what should be done and how it should get done, as long as those conflicts are brought to the surface and resolved. If you used team-based tools, like the ones outlined in this book, you can move through these conflicts quickly, building trust and respect as you go. You'll also be resolving the issues that stand in the way of gaining consensus on the project plan. Using a participative method as you work through storming will put you in good shape for the next team stage.

THE NORMING STAGE

If the team resolves its conflicts, it moves on to the next stage of development called norming. By this stage the project's goals, roles, and boundaries have been clarified and accepted by team members. They have taken ownership and accountability for getting the work done. You know you're in norming if you hear, "I can . . . ," "I will. . . ."

The norming stage usually emerges at the end of planning or in the beginning of the execution phase, depending on the complexity and controversy associated with the project and with your skills at working through the first two stages. In the norming stage, people get on with doing their own work. This stage comes as a big relief to both the project leader and the project team members.

In this stage, you'll need to hold regular team meetings so that team members can monitor progress and solve problems as they arise. You'll also want to focus on your team skills, such as:

✔ Holding effective meetings

✔ Practicing active listening

✔ Providing constructive feedback

✔ Resolving conflicts

✔ Making team decisions

The more team-based skills you have in your toolbox, the better you'll be at working through the norming stage.

If you've done a good job up to this point, working through the first two stages of team development, and if you continue to work in a productive, participatory fashion during the norming stage, you may just reach the next stage of team development, where the highest levels of performance are reached. This stage is called performing.

THE PERFORMING STAGE

In the performing stage the team becomes a true team, working in unison, supporting one another. The team, not the leader, manages the project. Team members make adjustments to keep the deliverables on track; they monitor progress and manage change. The team takes full ownership and accountability, not only for the project, but for the team dynamics as well. Key phrases are, "We can . . . ," "We will. . . ." When you hear those things, you'll know you've hit the upper registers for achieving results.

Don't relax too much during the performing stage. You'll still need to attend to the project management process as well as managing the dynamics of the team, but these should be second nature to you by this point. Remember to recognize accomplishments and celebrate successes.

Not many teams make it to the performing stage. In fact, some teams never make it past storming. However, if you're one of the successful ones, then you'll have an additional challenge on your hands, namely, disbanding of the team and facing the mourning stage of team development.

THE MOURNING STAGE

People don't like to leave a high-performing team because they feel good about themselves and what they've accomplished together. They have enjoyed being a member of a team and contributing to something larger than themselves. For most people, this is an infrequent experience that makes it difficult to let go. However, all projects by definition are temporary and so inevitably the peak experience must come to an end. At that point the team hits the mourning stage.

In the mourning stage it's important to both celebrate and to mourn. Celebration should have been a theme throughout the team process; otherwise you're unlikely to be in the mourning stage at all, but this is the time for a final celebration of the overall achievements of the team. Also, it's time for closure on the team process—saying good-bye to friends and associates. A closing ritual can be helpful to help bring a close to the project.

STAGES OF DEVELOPMENT AND PARTICIPATION

Hopefully, it's obvious by now that a directive approach to project management won't do much to help a team get through stages of team development. In fact, projects managed with a directive style often stall at forming. If the project leader is open to conflict, they may move on to storming and to a nominal norming stage, but that's the end of the journey. There's unlikely to be a high-performing team and there is unlikely to be much mourning when the project comes to an end.

In fact, with a directive approach the team hardly forms at all. Most of the interaction is between the project leader and individuals on the team. This allows very little opportunity for team members to collaborate amongst themselves and thus to form a team.

HIGH-PERFORMING TEAMS

Developing a high-performing team not only produces higher levels of performance, but it's also more fun to work on a high-performing team that works well and gets things done. (See Table 3.1.) If you're already on

TABLE 3.1 High-Performing Team Assessment						
1. Team member goals are aligned with the project's goals.	1	2	3	4	5	6
2. The team is focused on interdependent actions.	1	2	3	4	5	6
3. Team members participate in the planning and monitoring/control processes.	1	2	3	4	5	6
4. Decisions are made primarily by consensus.	1	2	3	4	5	6
5. The project leader and team members own the project plan and its execution.	1	2	3	4	5	6
6. Team members are empowered.	1	2	3	4	5	6
7. Conflicts arise and are resolved collaboratively.	1	2	3	4	5	6
8. People on the team feel listened to and supported.	1	2	3	4	5	6
9. Individual style differences are honored.	1	2	3	4	5	6
10. Individual needs are of concern to the team.	1	2	3	4	5	6
TOTAL (Add up your total score)						
AVERAGE (Total divided by 10)						

a project team, take a minute to do a quick inventory of how your team stacks up against the ten characteristics of high-performing teams. Rate your team on a scale of 1 to 6 where 1 = we never do this and 6 = we always do this. Then add up your total score. A perfect score would be 60. If you get a 60, you're probably lying! Then divide your total by 10 to get an average score. If your average is 4 or higher, you're doing extremely well, although there is always room for improvement. If your average is lower, don't despair. We've got a lot more material to cover that will help you improve your score.

Creating a high-performing team takes commitment on the part of the project leader to lead both the project management and team processes. Project leaders need to be <u>facilitators,</u> helping the team work through the steps of these processes. Here are some tips on being a <u>good facilitator:</u>

✔ Allow opportunity for equal participation by all team members.

✔ Maintain a safe environment.

✔ Acknowledge each person's contribution.

✔ Enforce the team ground rules.

✔ Focus on the team and project management processes, not the content.

✔ Respect each person as an individual.

✔ Resolve conflicts as they arise.

✔ Keep the group on track.

PROJECT LEADER SKILLS

Facilitation skills are just one set of skills that will be needed by the project leader and subproject team leaders if they want to create high-performing teams. In Table 3.2 rate your skills on a scale of 1 to 6

TABLE 3.2 Project Leader Skills Assessment						
1. Leading the team through the steps of the project management process	1	2	3	4	5	6
2. Leading the team through the stages of team development	1	2	3	4	5	6
3. Verbal-communication skills, both one-on-one and with a group, and written communication skills	1	2	3	4	5	6
4. People-management skills such as constructive feedback, conflict resolution, managing individual styles and personalities	1	2	3	4	5	6
5. Facilitation skills	1	2	3	4	5	6
6. Skills at interfacing across the organization and removing obstacles for the team	1	2	3	4	5	6
7. Ability to accept criticism, feedback, and inputs from others	1	2	3	4	5	6
8. Skilled in using team-based tools such as brainstorming, organizing, decision making, project management, conflict resolution, and so on.	1	2	3	4	5	6
9. Selling skills. The ability to promote and sell the project both within and outside the organization. Presentation skills.	1	2	3	4	5	6
10. Leadership skills	1	2	3	4	5	6
TOTAL (Add up your total score)						
AVERAGE (Total divided by 10)						

where 1 = my skills in this area are minimal and 6 = I do extremely well at this. Add up your total score. Then divide your total by 10 to get an average score. No matter what your score, you can always improve the way you manage projects.

A more extensive assessment of project leader skills can be found in Appendix A.

Chapter

4

Kicking Off the Project

The kick-off meeting is the team's first introduction to the project and it's the formal beginning of both the planning phase of the project management process and the forming stage of the team-development process.

KICK OFF AND THE TEAM PROCESS

During the forming stage, team members are wondering, "What is this project all about? How will it be run? Who are the other people on the team? Will this project be fun?" It's the project leader's job to help the people on the team answer these questions.

The kick-off meeting sets the tone for the entire project. Team members will be evaluating you as a project leader. How will you lead the team? What style will you use? Will you fight for the project? What are your strengths? Weaknesses? They are also evaluating the project. Is it meaningful? Does it matter to the organization? Does it matter to me? Is it doable? Does it make sense? Will it be a challenge? Will it be fun to do?

It's important to plan the kick-off meeting carefully so that you

66

kick off both the planning phase and the forming stage as productively as possible.

THE KICK-OFF MEETING SET-UP

Room

Reserve a large room. You'll need plenty of space for everyone to sit comfortably and move around because they will be working at the walls for team exercises. Try to find a room without too many windows. This cuts down on the distractions and also gives you more wall space to use.

Seating

If you have a small team of ten or less, you can seat everyone around a single round or rectangular table. If you have a larger group (more than ten people), then you'll either need a large rectangular table (like a boardroom table) or several round or rectangular tables (see Figure 4.1). Do not seat people in classroom style, where the chairs are lined up in rows that face forward. That configuration suits a lecture/directive approach, not a participative one. You'll want your kick-off meeting to be active, not passive, so make sure people are seated in groups that enhance rather than inhibit interaction.

Supplies

You'll need at least one easel with flip-chart paper and plenty of markers. Bring lots of self-stick notes (Post-it™ Notes) of various sizes and colors. These will be used for recording ideas or issues/concerns. Also bring masking tape so you can tape the flip-chart paper to the wall.

Note: These guidelines for meeting set-up should be used for all team meetings, not just the kick-off meeting.

67

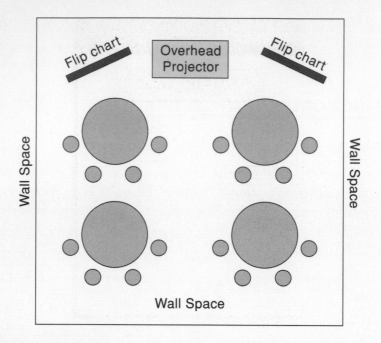

Figure 4.1 Room set-up.

THE PARKING LOT

Before the meeting starts, you should prepare a meeting parking lot. This is simply a piece of flip-chart paper with the heading, "Parking Lot" written across the top (see Figure 4.2).

It should be used as a discussion manager in all your project team meetings. Ideas, issues, or concerns that are raised during the meeting that cannot be answered immediately or that are outside the scope of the discussion are recorded on self-stick notes, and these are placed on the parking lot. At the end of the meeting, the parking lot is cleared by:

✔ Discarding items that have been addressed or are no longer an issue.

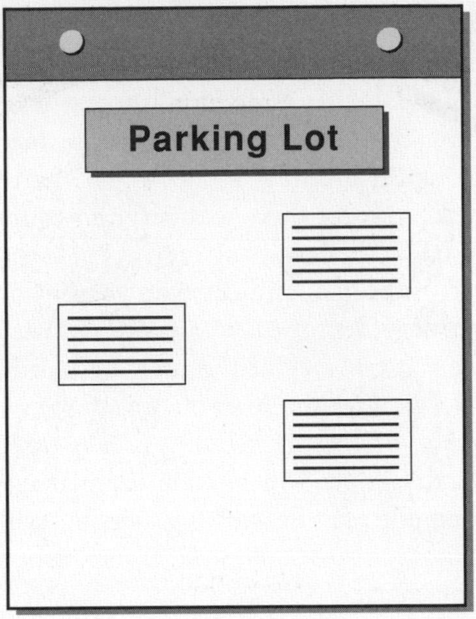

Figure 4.2 The parking lot.

✔ Transferring items to the issues list (which we'll cover shortly) for future action.

✔ Transferring items to a lessons-learned list (which will also be covered shortly).

✔ Placing items on the agenda for the next team meeting.

A parking lot is an essential tool in any participative process. It allows you to keep the meeting on track without discounting anyone's ideas or concerns. By recording and posting an idea or concern, the person whose idea it was is acknowledged, valued, and treated with respect. This builds trust and a feeling of safety while keeping the meeting on track.

69

WHO SHOULD BE INVITED?

Obviously you should invite your initial project team to the kick-off meeting. In addition, invite your sponsor, because one of the key things you'll do at the kick-off meeting is review the charter, and it will be helpful to have your sponsor there to answer any questions or address issues that are raised by the team.

If it's a large, important project, you may want to invite other members of the management team whose support is critical to the project's success. Their attendance at the meeting will be a sign of their support. If you do expand the kick-off meeting to include management-team members, divide the meeting into two segments; the first portion, the general session, will include the management-team invitees, and the second portion, the working meeting, will include just the project team and the sponsor. You'll need the sponsor to stay to answer questions about the charter.

MEETING AGENDA

An agenda should be issued before any meeting, and the kick-off meeting is no exception. The following is a suggested kick-off meeting agenda:

General session: (includes management team members)

✔ Introductions—Have all members introduce themselves, indicating which department they are representing.

✔ Review the charter—Review each section of the charter and ask for questions/concerns. This should be a high-level review. A more detailed review will be done during the working session.

Working session: (includes sponsor but not other management-team members)

✔ Introductions—Ask team members for more information on their backgrounds.

✔ Icebreaker—It's useful to include an icebreaker at this point in the meeting because you want the members of the project team to begin to get to know each other better.

✔ Review the charter in detail—Go over the charter again and discuss each section in depth. There may have been questions that team members were afraid to ask during the general session.

✔ Create a team contract—A team contract is an agreement between members of the project team on the guidelines for how the team will manage itself.

✔ Identify early issues—Are there any issues or action items that need immediate attention?

✔ Schedule future planning meetings—These are the meetings that will be used to work through the project planning activities.

Let's discuss each agenda item in more detail.

INTRODUCTIONS

Introductions are important because they help people get to know one another. During the management session, have all members introduce themselves, providing their names and the department they represent. During the working session, ask all members to introduce themselves again, this time explaining what they do and providing the team with a description of their background. This will help the team identify what each member brings to the table that could be useful for the project. It will also help the team begin the process of team formation.

If people in the group already know one another, it's still useful to do introductions. You might ask people to share why they think they have been asked to join the project. You might ask them to share something about themselves that is not too personal. Here are some questions that you might ask:

✔ Where in the world would you like to go that you have never been before?

✔ What is your most unusual hobby?

✔ What is the most exciting thing you've ever done?

✔ What did you want to be when you were growing up?

Keep the questions light. Do not embarrass anyone but begin the process of breaking the ice.

THE ICEBREAKER

One of your goals in the forming stage of team development is to help people to feel comfortable as a part of the team. One way to do that is to include an icebreaker in the kick-off meeting. The icebreaker you choose should

✔ Promote interactions between the participants.

✔ Not make people feel uncomfortable.

✔ Reveal something about the person and/or group that is relevant to the project.

✔ Be fun.

✔ Be short.

An example of a great icebreaker is called the Diversity Game. In addition to breaking the ice, it profiles team member and overall project team thinking styles. (Developed by Applied Creativity, the Diversity Game can be purchased from our web site at www.projectresults.com.) Using a deck of cards that contains 64 different thinking styles, team members are asked to assemble a hand of three cards that describes their thinking-style strengths. Then the thinking styles of the team are profiled to identify areas of strength and weakness. This is an excellent example of an icebreaker because it gets people up and talking to one another quickly (they get to swap cards with others in the room), but it also provides valuable information about team members and the team as a whole. If there are deficiencies in the thinking styles that will be needed to do the project, the project leader can identify these weaknesses early in the process. See Appendix B for more information on thinking styles. The Diversity Game is just one example of an icebreaker that meets the criteria for icebreakers already described and that helps the team move through the forming stage.

REVIEW THE CHARTER

It's important that everyone understand the expectations for the project that have been captured in the charter. Provide copies of the charter for both team members and invited guests. Have the sponsor review the charter with the management team guests to get their inputs and concerns. The sponsor should address their concerns or issues during the meeting, if possible. If they cannot be addressed, the project leader should put them on the issues list for resolution at a later date.

When the management guests have left the meeting, review the charter again with the project team:

- ✔ It's helpful to prepare a poster-sized copy of the charter and tape it to the wall. That will help everyone on the team follow the review process.
- ✔ As you review each section, ask for questions, suggested changes, and additions. Record the questions, issues, ideas, and inputs on self-stick notes and place them on the charter or on a piece of flip-chart paper.

✔ As the sponsor addresses each issue or question, write the response on another self-stick note and attach it to the first. If you don't do this, after the sponsor leaves the meeting, either you or the team will forget what the answer was or you'll have different perceptions of the answer.

✔ Place any unanswered questions on the issues list for follow-up after the meeting.

You'll probably find that some of the questions or concerns will relate to whether or not the project is realistic and doable. These questions, such as, "Can we make the deadline date?" or "Is this technically feasible?" will be addressed during the planning process, and you should not attempt to answer them now. On the other hand, unless the concerns are addressed in some fashion, the team may not be willing to move forward. Explain to the team that these are valid concerns and that they will be addressed as you move through the planning process. If, after planning, the team decides that it's not possible to meet the expectations as outlined in the charter, then you'll take the planning data back to the sponsor for a resolution. The planning process is designed to answer the question, "Can we accomplish what is asked of us in the charter, within the limits defined?" Therefore, it's not necessary to challenge the doability of the charter at the charter review stage. The purpose of the charter review is to understand what is required from the project from the sponsor's point of view. In addition, what seems unrealistic may prove to be possible once the team has a chance to work through the details of planning.

THE TEAM CONTRACT

After the charter is reviewed, you'll need to create a team contract, a set of guidelines that everyone on the team will agree to follow.

Anyone who has worked on a team has experienced team problems of one sort or another, such as team members showing up late for meetings, not coming prepared, and so on. The team contract is a tool that will help the team avoid some of these problems from occurring instead of waiting for them to happen and then reacting to them. The team contract is a set of guidelines or ground rules for team member behavior. Some examples of team ground rules are:

- ✔ Keep team issues within the team unless the team agrees otherwise.
- ✔ Give everyone the opportunity for equal participation.
- ✔ Practice active, effective listening skills.
- ✔ Make decisions based on data whenever possible.
- ✔ Get input from the entire team before a decision is made.
- ✔ Seek to understand the interests and desires of each party involved before arriving at answers or solutions.
- ✔ Meetings will begin and end on time.
- ✔ Team members will come to the meetings prepared.

There are two methods for creating and getting agreement on a set of team ground rules.

Method A

One way to create a team contract is to start with a sample contract and then have team members participate in modifying it to fit their experiences and concerns. A sample team contract has been provided in Appendix C. Divide the team into subgroups of three to four people and assign each group one or more of the sections in the sample team contract to modify. It's a good idea to print the sections of the team contract on overhead transparencies and then let the groups make the changes, using markers, directly on the transparencies. This will allow them to share their changes with the group.

Method B

Another approach to developing a team contract is to:

- ✔ Ask each team member to write down all the types of team problems he or she has experienced on prior projects. Give team members markers and self-stick notes for recording their ideas.

- ✔ After team members have recorded their ideas, ask them to place them on a piece of banner paper that has been taped to the wall.

- ✔ Ask the team to sort the problems (while standing at the wall), placing similar types of problems together. It's best to have the team do this in silence.

- ✔ After the ideas have been organized, have the group define a category heading for each grouping. The category name should be a complete thought, such as "Run meetings efficiently." (This brainstorming/organizing process is called affinity diagramming. Generic instructions on how to do affinity diagramming are included in Chapter 11.)

After the categories have been named, divide the team into subgroups of three to four people. Assign each group one or more of the categories. Ask them to write guidelines based on the ideas in their category, recording them on flip-chart paper so they can be shared with the entire group.

When all subgroups have completed their section of the team contract, using either method A or method B, ask them to share their changes with the group. (If they used transparencies, you'll need an overhead projector.) Ask for concerns or issues from the rest of the group as each subgroup reviews its ground rules. Then ask for consensus on each section. When the review is complete and you have a contract that everyone can live with, ask each person to sign the document. Placing their signatures on something creates a stronger commitment for people than simple verbal agreement.

76

Note: It's not a good idea to ask for signatures when you work in a culture where people are afraid of getting blamed when and if something goes wrong. Remember, your intent should be to build individual responsibility toward the project, and to build trust between you and the team and between members of the team. In a fear-based culture, dispense with the signatures.

Once you have your team ground rules, it's time to begin the steps of planning the project. Canvas the group to see if there are any early issues that must be addressed before you begin the planning process. If there are, add them to the issues list.

SCHEDULE PLANNING MEETINGS

Before you begin planning, set up a schedule for future planning meetings so that everyone can set aside the time required to complete the project plan. The amount of time you'll need to devote to planning will depend on the following factors:

- ✔ Number of people involved in the project team—The more people involved, the more time you'll need to plan.

- ✔ The complexity of the technology—The more complex the deliverables you must create, the more time it will take to plan.

- ✔ The magnitude of the project—The broader the objectives of the project, the more work there will be and, therefore, the more planning you'll require.

- ✔ The experience of the team—Teams that have experience in similar types of projects will need less time to plan than teams with people who are new to your type of project. Also, teams that are experienced in project management require less planning time than inexperienced teams.

77

✔ The amount of historical data available from past projects—
The more information you have about how similar projects
were planned and the actual results they experienced, the easier it will be for you to plan yours.

SAMPLE KICK-OFF MEETINGS

Before we move on to the planning phase, let's take one more look at
the kick-off process. We're going to eavesdrop on a kick-off meeting
that doesn't exactly set the right tone for the project. Ron, the project
leader, is about to conduct his kick-off meeting. See if you can identify
what he's doing wrong.

"Welcome to the kick-off meeting for our project. As you all
know, this project is really important for future earnings growth, so you
should all feel very proud to be on the team. I expect that you'll give
this project your complete and undivided attention. Because we all
know each other let's not waste time on introductions. I'm handing out
the charter document that our sponsor, Sara, provided. If you have any
questions, just let me know and I'll pass them on to her." There is silence in the room as people read the document. Larry raises a concern
about the deadlines and Ron replies, "Sure, it's a stretch but I know we
can do it if we pull together. I've put together a schedule that I think is
doable. I'll hand it out as soon as we get through this charter. Anyone
else have a concern?"

Bonnie asks a question and Ron replies, "That's not really relevant
to the discussion at hand; I think we'd better move on."

Obviously Ron is not a model for what to do right. Let's examine
some of the things that Ron has already done wrong:

He has not included introductions or an icebreaker in the meeting, so people don't have a chance to get to know one another.

He has not had the team create a team contract.

He shows no tolerance for challenges to the charter document.

He has created a schedule without team participation.

He has not set up a parking lot to park ideas, issues, or concerns that are not relevant to the discussion at hand.

In order to get the results Ron needs for the project, he's going to have to make some changes to his approach. Maybe he can learn from Sam, a project leader who uses the CORE PM approach.

Sam starts his kick-off meeting by saying, "Although we all know one another, let's spend a few minutes catching up on what each of us has been doing lately, and then I'd like to play a thinking-styles game. This will provide us a profile of our own and our team's thinking styles. I've set up a parking lot so we won't lose any of the ideas, concerns, or issues that you have. We will address how we'll handle each one before the end of the meeting.

"After we profile our thinking styles, I'd like to create a team contract that we all feel we can live by while we work on this project together. This will help us to avoid unnecessary problems and conflicts about how we'll work together as a team.

"I've worked with the sponsor on the charter, which I sent out to you ahead of time. I'd like to collect your comments, questions, concerns, and ideas about the charter. We'll record each one on a self-stick note and place it on the banner paper I've placed on the wall. Once we resolve any issues we have with the charter, we'll begin creating the project plan together, as a team."

Sam is acting as a facilitator rather than a director. He encourages team participation. He solicits issues and ideas. Sam treats each individual on the team with respect. He listens to their concerns and makes sure that each one gets addressed. In this way he validates for each team member that his concerns are real and important.

Sam is paying attention to both the team process and the project management process, and he is involving the team in the project. He is a smart project leader and smart project leaders involve the team in the project.

THE PLANNING PROCESS

Before we dive into project planning, let's look at how the planning activities that you'll need to do for your project are connected to the unique characteristics of projects that we discussed in Chapter 1. (See Table 4.1.)

We'll cover these planning activities over the next five chapters. (See Table 4.2.)

Don't be frightened by the number of activities involved in planning. It's really quite straightforward, and it gets much easier with practice. Besides, you'll be getting lots of help from the members of your team. That's one of the great benefits of having them participate.

TABLE 4.1 Planning Activities vs. Characteristics of Projects	
Characteristic of Projects	*Planning Activities Required*
Temporary endeavor	✔ The team must be recruited
	✔ The project must be organized
	✔ The start and end dates must be identified and confirmed through a project schedule
	✔ A budget must be created
Unique output	✔ The customer requirements for the final deliverable must be clearly defined
	✔ What's included and not included in the project must be defined
	✔ A description of the final deliverable must be written
No predefined work assignment	✔ Who will do what must be decided
	✔ Accountability must be assigned

TABLE 4.2 Planning Activities by Chapter		
Segment	*Activities*	*Chapter in the Book*
Define the scope	✔ Validate what the customer expects from the project ✔ Clearly define the final deliverable ✔ Define what's included and not included in the project ✔ Identify all stakeholders	5. Planning the Scope
Organize the work	✔ Make sure you have the right people on the team ✔ Make sure all stakeholders have some type of representation on the team ✔ Break the final deliverable down into manageable parts ✔ Assign each part to a team member	6. Organizing the Project
Assess risk	✔ Figure out what might go wrong and find ways to prevent problems from occurring	7. Assessing Risk
Develop a project schedule	✔ Schedule all the work that must be accomplished	8. Developing a Schedule
Develop a budget	✔ Create a budget for people's time commitments to the project ✔ Develop a spending budget	9. Developing a Budget
Write the project plan	✔ Gather the procedures that will be used to make changes to the plan ✔ Compile the information developed during planning into a formal project plan and get it approved	10. Assembling the Project Plan

CONTENT AND PROCESS CHECK

Before you move on to planning the project, do a content and process check to make sure you haven't missed anything during kick off.

- ❏ Did you issue an agenda before the kick-off meeting?
- ❏ Was everyone included in the kick-off meeting who could have benefited from being there?
- ❏ Did you ask each person to introduce himself or herself?
- ❏ Did you include an icebreaker to help the team move through the forming stage of development?
- ❏ Did you invite the sponsor to the kick off so he or she could answer questions about the charter?
- ❏ Did you review the charter in depth? Did you record questions and answers so they were visible to the entire team?
- ❏ Did you facilitate rather than dominate the meeting?
- ❏ Did you encourage participation in the kick-off meeting?
- ❏ Have you scheduled the planning meetings?

MOVING ON

Now you're ready to move on to planning. Just as the kick off was a participatory process, planning also needs to be done in a participatory fashion, with the project leader acting as a facilitator for the project management activities outlined in this book. Planning will challenge your team skills because as we move into planning, we also move into the storming stage of team development. However, the storming stage will be less intense and more productive if the team is fully involved in making the planning decisions for the project.

Planning the Scope

At the conclusion of the initiation phase, the sponsor approves the charter, which outlines what the project should accomplish and what resources will be available.

The charter is the vision for the project. It's the expectations and sometimes even the dreams of the customer and sponsor. What is requested in the charter may or may not be doable. It's during project planning that the feasibility of the charter is determined. Project planning is about reality: what can be done, how long will it take, who will do what, and how much it will cost. The charter addresses the questions "why" and "what." The project plan addresses the questions "who," "how," "when," and "how much." It's not unusual that the reality of what can be accomplished with the resources that are available is different than the expectations as they are outlined in the charter. Planning will help you sort out what's possible from what's not.

However, you should approach planning with the intent of meeting the charter expectations. Sometimes what looks like an impossibility, with a little creative thinking, turns out to be possible after all. Then again, sometimes it turns out not to be possible, and either the expectations must be adjusted or more resources added to the project.

Planning also defines a game plan for how the deliverables of the project will be created: what will be produced, when, by whom, for how much money. This detailed game plan is what you'll use to execute the project.

The first thing you need to do as you begin planning is nail down the scope of the project: what will be produced for the customer. The scope is the most important element of a project because it drives all the resource requirements. If you have a broad scope, you need more resources. If you have a narrow scope, you need fewer resources.

The customer defines scope, so the first issue is to make sure you've identified the right customer for your project.

DEFINING THE CUSTOMER

There are two types of customers that need to be considered in every project: the end customer (end user) and the project customer. (See Table 5.1.)

The project customer is the customer who receives the final deliverable from the project. He or she may or may not be the end user of the deliverable. In our fulfillment example, the project customer is the business-process manager, Ken. The people who will be working in the fulfillment center are the end users of the fulfillment process.

Do you need to worry about the requirements of the end user? Absolutely. In order to design our fulfillment process, we must know what the end user requires to do his job effectively and efficiently. End user requirements are often gathered before the project begins, as part

TABLE 5.1 **Characteristics of Customers**	
Type of Customer	*Characteristics*
End Customer (end user)	✔ Ultimate user of the product, service, process, or plan being developed or improved
	✔ In the case of a process, the end customer is the person or group that will run the process
Project Customer	✔ The person or group who will receive the final deliverable from the project

of a market research effort or the product concept definition. If the end user requirements are not defined before the project begins or if they're not available to the project team, then you will need to gather them before you design the final deliverable. Often these requirements can be assessed in more depth during the execution phase. In some instances, however, you will need to go out and collect these requirements during planning:

✔ When the end user requirements have not been assessed at all
✔ When the project customer does not have a clear understanding of the end user requirements
✔ When the end user requirements may differ significantly from the project customer requirements

The processes by which requirements are collected, either for the end user or for the project customer, are very similar. Therefore, we're going to talk about assessing what the project customer's needs and requirements are; he or she is the customer you'll hand-off your final deliverable to and is the person who will typically evaluate the project. If you need to collect end user requirements, use the process described for the project customer.

CUSTOMER NEED

The first thing you'll want to validate is the customer's need, which is the problem the project customer is trying to solve. Although the need should have been defined in the charter, you'll need to make sure you understand the need thoroughly. The best way to do this is to visit the customer and actually experience the problem he or she is facing.

The reason you explore the customer need is to make sure you understand the root cause or causes of the problem that has led the customer to request the final deliverable, which is the customer's perception of the solution to his problem. Customers often come to us with stated solutions. "I need a caplet formulation for the new aspirin product." It may be that the caplet formulation is the best solution for the problem that the customer or his or her customers are experiencing. On the other hand, you may find there is an alternative solution that might work even better. By exploring the need, you get beyond the stated solutions to the real problem.

Visit the customer and ask him or her to show you, if possible, the problem or problems that are being experienced. If you can't see the problem interview the customer, so that you understand the problem. You may find you'll have to probe the customer to get to the real problem he is facing. For example, if Ken, the fulfillment process manager, were to say that his need is for an in-house fulfillment process, then you might ask, "What are the problems with the current system that an in-house system is supposed to relieve?" The in-house process is a solution. Long cycle times and inaccurate shipments are the problems.

Here are some suggestions for helping to probe the customer on the real problem he is facing:

✔ What effect does this problem have on the business?

✔ Why do you think this problem exists?

✔ If we deliver the solution you have requested, what problems would go away?

What you're really doing is probing the customer's assumptions about the solution or final deliverable that he or she has requested. Assumptions are things we believe to be true. For example, Ken assumes (believes) that long cycle times and inaccurate shipments are a result of having an outside vendor manage the fulfillment operation. He has come to the conclusion that bringing the fulfillment process in house will solve his problem. This assumption may or may not be true.

You can't test an assumption unless you know what it is. When you validate the customer need you make sure the assumptions that are held by the customer are true or the best approximation of the truth available at the time.

There are more quantitative methods for getting at the real problem and making sure you've got the right solution to that problem. (The solution is the final deliverable you've been asked to produce.) These problem-solving methodologies can be employed to analyze the problem and select the best possible solution. (MartinTate has a three-stage method that is described in Appendix D.) If you're unsure of whether you have identified the true problem, you should consider using a problem-solving methodology before you proceed any further with the project.

What's the danger of not understanding the customer's needs or assumptions? If in our fulfillment example, the long cycle times and inaccurate shipments have nothing to do with the outside vendor, but instead have to do with inaccurate orders coming in through the customer sales process, we will have designed and installed an in-house fulfillment process and we will not have solved the problem. This is not a good thing. Therefore, it's best to get to the root problem(s) before you get too far down the road of planning how you'll produce the final deliverable that's supposed to solve the problem.

THE FINAL DELIVERABLE

Once you've assessed the customer need, you're in a position to validate the final deliverable. Is the final deliverable the best possible solution to the project customer's problems? If not, you need to go back to the sponsor and customer and discuss options. Propose an alternative solution that would better address the problem.

The final deliverable isn't a magic bullet. It isn't going to completely solve the customer's problem. However, it should at least be a partial solution to the problem (see Figure 5.1). In order to solve the entire problem, the customer may need more than one project and thus more than one final deliverable.

Although you need to define the problem that the customer is experiencing, you are not accountable to solve that problem. What you are accountable for is delivering a final deliverable that satisfies the cus-

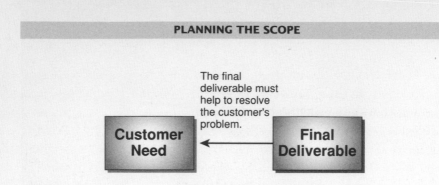

Figure 5.1 The final deliverable satisfies a need.

tomer. However, if you haven't at least alleviated the customer's problem, then the likelihood that the customer will be satisfied with the final deliverable, even if it's exactly what they asked for, is not very high. Therefore, take the time to define the problem and make sure your final deliverable will help them to resolve that problem. Then you can move on to the next step of defining how the customer will determine their level of satisfaction with the final deliverable after they receive it. Satisfying the customer is the aim of any project, and customers are satisfied when their criteria for satisfaction, called customer acceptance criteria, are met. How do you know what the customer's criteria for acceptance of the final deliverable are? You ask.

CUSTOMER ACCEPTANCE CRITERIA

Customer acceptance criteria are the criteria the customer will use to evaluate whether they are satisfied with the final deliverable that you produce. Because the purpose of the project is to satisfy the customer, it's important to know their criteria for satisfaction. These criteria, also referred to as CAC, become your target for the project. If you hit the target, the customer will be satisfied. Without them, you don't have a clear end goal for the deliverable, and that always spells trouble (see Figure 5.2).

The best approach to defining the CAC is to conduct an interview with the customer. Ask them to imagine that you are delivering the final deliverable to them and they are beginning to use it. Ask

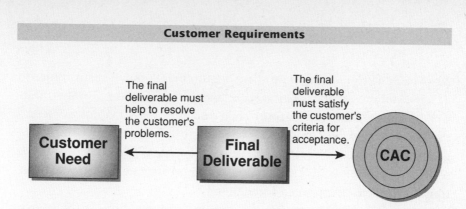

Figure 5.2 CAC are used to measure the final deliverable.

them what three or four main performance characteristics of the final deliverable would cause them to rate that deliverable as satisfactory. One of the characteristics that Ken, our fulfillment manager, defines is a short cycle time.

If the criteria that the customer defines are not measurable, probe to see if there is a way to measure them. Ken explains that to him, a short cycle time means one that is less than 48 hours. This is a measurable characteristic and one that we can use for a target for our work. A criterion that says, "the fulfillment process is streamlined" does not make a clear target. A criterion that an order can be picked and packed in less than 60 minutes is a goal that's clear.

CUSTOMER REQUIREMENTS

While you are interviewing the customer about the CAC, it's a good time to validate and expand on the customer's requirements for the final deliverable. Customer requirements include any features and functions of the final deliverable. A feature is a physical characteristic of the final deliverable. An example of a feature for our fulfillment process would be including bar codes on all inventory items. A function is an action or work that the final deliverable will perform. A function of our fulfillment process would be that inventory levels in the accounting program are automatically adjusted.

Customer requirements should have been outlined in the charter.

Now it's time to expand upon these requirements. Ask the customer to describe all the features they require and every function they are interested in (See Table 5.2). Capture each one on a self-stick note. After all the features and functions have been identified, ask the customer to group them into three categories: must have, highly desirable, and nice to have. This will enable you to match each category to a level of customer satisfaction you intend to deliver.

Check to make sure that the features and functions in the must-have category are aligned with the CAC and that you aren't missing any requirements (see Figure 5.3). Next check the highly desirable category to decide which of these, if any, can be included in the final deliverable. Remember that the list of features and functions included in the final deliverable will drive the resource requirements for the project, so you'll only be able to add as many features and functions as you have the money to fund. Later on, you'll need to explore the requirements in more depth (converting them to technical specifications), as you get ready to actually design the final deliverable, but for now, all you need to do is develop an accurate plan that sets realistic expectations about what will be produced.

TABLE 5.2 Features and Functions Categories	
Category of Final Deliverable Features and Functions	*How Delivering the Features and Functions Relates to Customer Satisfaction*
Must have	✔ The final deliverable will meet the CAC
	✔ The customer will be satisfied with the final deliverable
Highly desirable	✔ The final deliverable will exceed the CAC
	✔ The customer will be delighted with the final deliverable
Nice to have	✔ There are usually not enough resources to include nice to have features; however, if they are included, the customer will be delighted

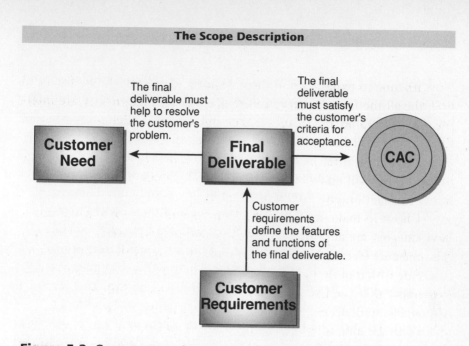

Figure 5.3 Customer requirements and the final deliverable.

THE SCOPE DESCRIPTION

After you have defined the customer requirements, you're ready to write a description of the final deliverable. This is called the scope description. The purpose of the scope description is to fully describe what will be produced, so that when the customer reads it, he or she can say, "Yes, this is what I want," or "No, you've missed something here." The scope description is a communication tool to ensure that what you are producing is what the customer and sponsor want you to produce.

The scope description will probably only be a couple of paragraphs. You can attach the list of requirements to the description to document the features and functions that will be included in the final deliverable. If a drawing or diagram would help describe the final deliverable, include it. Anything that communicates what your final product will be is helpful here.

Suppose you were commissioned to plan a celebration for a new product line that your company has recently launched successfully. The final deliverable is a dinner/dance to be held for selected employees and their invited guests. The scope description for this project might start out as follows:

> The product launch celebration will be held on September 15th at the Magnolia Plantation. There will be no more than 100 invited guests (employees and key suppliers). They, in turn, will be allowed to invite one guest of their own. Therefore, the total number of attendees will not exceed 200. The celebration will start at 7:00 P.M. with an outside reception and then an inside catered dinner. There will be 30 minutes of speeches after dinner. A dance band will be provided for the evening entertainment. The dinner/dance will end at 12 P.M. Dress will be business attire. The décor will be in the style of. . . .

The scope description would continue, describing the critical features and functions related to our final deliverable, the dinner/dance. The project customer, the VP of marketing, would review the scope description to make sure that you were on the right track as you progressed with your planning activities.

SCOPE BOUNDARIES

After we describe the final deliverable, it's important that we clarify what's included and what's not included in the scope of the project. These are the scope boundaries for the project (see Figure 5.4). By defining the scope boundaries, you'll avoid confusion about what's included and excluded from the project and do a better job of steering a straight course to your goal of satisfying the customer.

To define the scope boundaries, write the name of the final deliverable on a piece of banner paper that has been taped to the wall and draw a large rectangle around it. This is your scope fence. Inside the fence, list the major tasks that will be required to produce the final de-

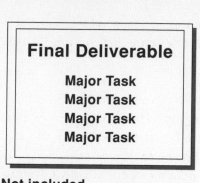

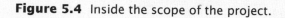

Figure 5.4 Inside the scope of the project.

liverable. For example, in the product launch dinner/dance project, getting entertainment, having the dinner catered, and inviting guests are all major tasks that would be included in your project.

Next, below the border of the fence, list anything that is outside the scope of your project. In our product launch project, transportation to the dinner/dance would be outside the scope of the project.

Now that you have defined what's inside and what's outside the scope, you'll need to consider any overlaps in scope (see Figure 5.5). One of the authors worked on a project that was chartered to redesign an expensive product part in order to reduce manufacturing costs. The team worked for 18 months and finally achieved its goal. Unbeknownst to them, another project team, which was working to reduce the overall cost of the product, eliminated the expensive part from the product design! So the first project team accomplished its goal—reducing the cost of the part—but it no longer mattered. The part was history. Don't let this happen to you. Find out what other projects are planned or in progress that might impact your project. (Your sponsor should be able to help here.) Draw a circle that overlaps with your scope fence and list any overlapping projects in the circle.

To complete your scope boundaries, you need to define exactly when the execution phase of the project will end. Let's take our product

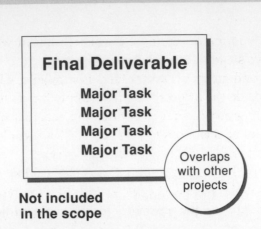

Figure 5.5 Overlaps in scope.

launch dinner/dance example; when is the final deliverable actually complete? At 12:00 P.M. when the dance is over? After the clean-up for the dance has been completed? After the bills have been paid?

Deciding when a project like the fulfillment project ends can be even trickier. At what point have we demonstrated that the process performs as promised? After one trial run? Two? A pilot run of a week? There are no right answers to these questions, but it's important that you define the end point up front, so that it's clear to everyone when the final deliverable has been delivered.

STAKEHOLDERS

Stakeholders, as we discussed in the charter section, are people or groups that will be affected by the project. There are four main types of stakeholders: customers, suppliers, other projects, and other groups. Customer stakeholders are ones who will be affected by the final deliverable. This includes the project customer because the customer is the recipient of the final deliverable. There may be other groups that are also affected by the final deliverable. For example, the final deliverable may change the way work is performed or it may increase the volume of work. The worker's union would, therefore, be a customer stakeholder.

The second group of stakeholders is suppliers, which are persons or groups outside the project team that supply inputs to the project.

The third group includes any other projects that would be affected by your project or that would affect yours. These would be included in the overlaps section of the scope-boundaries chart.

Finally, we have other groups that are affected by the work. These are usually people involved in the project, like the resource managers who will be supplying people and/or money to the project.

Create a table like the one shown in Figure 5.6. List each stakeholder group, the type of stakeholder, and how they will be affected by the project. Leave the rest of the columns blank. We'll fill them in later on in the process.

CONTENT AND PROCESS CHECK

Before you finalize the scope section, it's useful to do a content and process check to make sure you haven't missed anything.

❏ Have you identified the problem that the final deliverable is supposed to help to solve?

❏ Will the final deliverable help to resolve the problem(s) the customer is experiencing?

STAKEHOLDER FORM					
Stakeholder Group	Type of Stakeholder	How Affected by the Project?	Key Stakeholder?	Team Status	Team Member Liason

Figure 5.6 Stakeholder form.

❑ Does the scope description accurately describe what will be produced by the project?

❑ Is there consensus on what will be produced by the project?

❑ Have you captured the list of customer requirements?

❑ Are the customer's acceptance criteria written from the customer's point of view? Are they measurable?

❑ Is the end point for the project clearly defined?

❑ Have all groups that will be affected by the project been identified? Have all groups that will affect the project been identified?

❑ Have any project overlaps been identified?

❑ Did the team actively participate in defining the scope of the project? If not, why not?

THE PROJECT PLAN DOCUMENT

Now, you're ready to compile the scope section of the project plan. The project plan is a document that communicates the plan for the project to the outside world. As we discuss each section of planning, we'll talk about what to include in the project plan document.

The scope section of the project plan includes the following:

✔ The restated definition of the customer need

✔ A detailed description of the final deliverable, including the features and functions that will be included

✔ The customer's criteria for acceptance of the final deliverables, in measurable terms, if possible

✔ A description of the scope boundaries

✔ A description of the end point for the final deliverable

✔ A list of stakeholders and a description of how they will be affected by the project

The project plan document is not issued until after all the planning activities have been completed, but you'll want to review the scope section with your sponsor, customer, and key stakeholders before moving on to the next section of planning, because scope is the foundation for what follows. Hopefully, they'll provide validation that you're on the right track or else they'll let you know you need to make some adjustments before you go too much further.

Chapter 6

Organizing the Project

O nce you've defined the scope of your project, you now have to figure out how you're going to get the work done. This requires some project organization.

BREAKING DOWN THE FINAL DELIVERABLE

The first step to getting organized requires breaking down the final deliverable into manageable work units, which is a chunk of work that can be done by a single person. When that unit of work, also known as a work process, is complete, an output is produced. (A work process is a set of steps that produces an output or deliverable.) For example, if you were to install shelves in a warehouse, the output of the shelving work process would be installed shelves. In a project, the output is called an interim deliverable. Each interim deliverable is an output of a unit of work, and it also acts as an input to another work process that produces another interim deliverable, which in turn is an input to a work process, until eventually you produce your final deliverable (see Figure 6.1). This chain of interconnected or interdependent deliver-

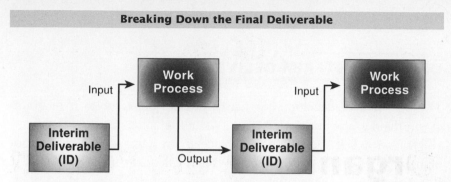

Figure 6.1 Interim deliverables and work processes.

ables is called an input/output chain. In our fulfillment example, the installed shelves are an input to the next interim deliverable, the completed warehouse.

So, an interim deliverable is an output that is created as a result of a work process that leads, through a chain of interim deliverables, to the final deliverable. If the work doesn't lead to the final deliverable, then you don't need it. Everything you do in your project should eventually lead to the final deliverable for the customer.

Think about building a house. The final deliverable is the house. The interim deliverables include the excavated lot, the building permits, the foundation, the frame, the interior walls, and so on. Each of these outputs was created as a result of a work process done by one or more people and each interim deliverable is necessary to the creation of the final deliverable, the custom house.

Breaking the project down into interim deliverables is the best way to create a manageable unit of work that can be assigned to an individual team member. A manageable unit of work is characterized as follows:

- ✔ It is not so big that a single person can't oversee that the work gets done.
- ✔ It can be performed by one person or by a small group of people.

DEFINING INTERIM DELIVERABLES

The best way to develop your list of interim deliverables is to brainstorm them with your project team. Write the name of the final deliverable(s) on a self-stick note and place it on a piece of flip-chart or banner paper attached to the wall. Then ask team members to write down the name of each interim deliverable that will be produced in order to create that final deliverable. Write each interim deliverable on a self-stick note and place it on the paper.

Tip: Don't worry about having the interim deliverables in any particular order. You'll organize them in the next step.

Remember, a deliverable is a thing (a noun) or the completion of a task or activity (verb, past tense). Installed shelving is a thing. The dinner/dance is a completed activity.

You may find that some interim deliverables represent very large chunks of work. Try to break these down further (see Figure 6.2). For example, suppose you have to produce a business plan as an interim deliverable for your project. You could break this down into a series of interim deliverables such as an outline, the rough draft, final text

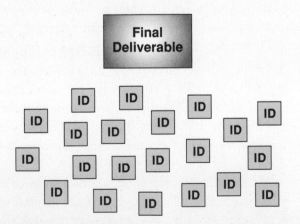

Figure 6.2 Break down the final deliverable into interim deliverables.

100

draft, and final draft with illustrations. The smaller the unit of work, the easier it is to manage. However, if you make the unit too small you'll clutter your project plan with too much detail. So, what's the right amount? Well, you'll learn that with experience, but for beginners, it's best to err on the side of too many interim deliverables rather than too few.

CREATING SUBPROJECTS

Once you've identified the interim deliverables, you'll need to assign each of them to one of the subdivisions of your project, your subprojects. If you recall, a subproject is a subset of the main project that is assigned to someone on the team to oversee.

In small projects, the work of the subproject is done by a member of the main project team. In large projects, a team of people may be required to do the work of a subproject, and so a subproject team leader is assigned to oversee the work of the subproject team. This subproject team leader is also a member of the main project team. The subproject team leader may or may not do some of the subproject work himself or herself, just as the project leader may or may not do work on the main project.

The role of the subproject team leader is basically the same as that of the project leader, except the subproject leader heads up the subproject and the project leader heads up the main project. The subproject leader is accountable for making sure his or her team completes the work of the subproject as required by the main project team. To be accountable means that the subproject leader must make sure that the work gets done correctly. It does not mean the subproject leader has to do the work himself.

Subproject teams follow the same phases and do most of the same activities as the main project. The following is the general sequence of how the subprojects and main project team work through the activities of planning a project. (See Table 6.1.)

TABLE 6.1 Subproject Planning	
Planning Activity	*Sequence of Planning for Large Projects*
Scope plan	✔ The scope definition is defined at the main project level first. Then, after the project is organized, the subprojects define the scope for the subprojects.
Risk assessment	✔ The subprojects usually do the risk assessment first and then the results are brought to the main project team to incorporate into the overall risk assessment.
Resource planning— schedule	✔ The main project schedule is drafted and then each subproject creates a subproject schedule. These schedules are then brought back to the main project where the final project schedule is modified, if necessary.
Resource planning— budgets	✔ The subprojects estimate their budgets first and then they are collated into a budget for the main project.

DEFINING THE SUBPROJECTS

How do you figure out what subprojects you should have? The best method is to group the interim deliverables together into similar types of work or work that requires similar types of skills (see Figure 6.3). Do this by moving the self-stick notes of the interim deliverables you developed in the last step into groups. (Group the interim deliverables in horizontal, not vertical groups. This will make it easier to create the subproject tree diagram for the project later on.) Usually, grouping work this way matches pretty closely the departments or resource areas in an organization, such as marketing, design, development, and so on. Each group of interim deliverables becomes a subproject.

Tip: Don't worry if you have a few outliers that don't seem to fit into any subproject. We'll deal with those shortly.

Next, label each group or subproject. The subproject name

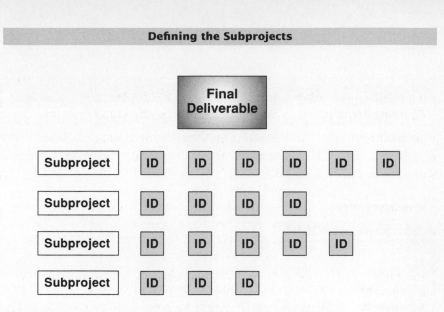

Figure 6.3 Group interim deliverables into subprojects.

should be short, two or three words at most, and should summarize the type of work that will be done in that subproject. For example, marketing, design, and engineering are typical names of product development subprojects. Once you have named the subprojects, review any outlier interim deliverables to see if they fit into any of the existing subprojects. If not, put them into a subproject entitled project management. In addition to outliers, this subproject contains the products of the project management process such as the project plan and the close-out report. The project management subproject is the accountability of the project leader.

Place the final deliverable in one of the subprojects. It's often created by the project leader in which case it would belong in the project management subproject, but sometimes the final deliverable is actually created in one of the subprojects.

Review the interim deliverables for each subproject. Are there any deliverables missing? If so, add them to the appropriate subproject. Make sure you don't have any duplicates.

Note: You can't have two subprojects producing the same interim deliverable. If two subprojects will work on the interim deliverable, break the deliverable down into two separate deliverables and place each in the appropriate subproject.

When you've finished defining the deliverables, number each one with a unique, consecutive number. It doesn't matter where you start or the order of the numbering, as long as each deliverable has a unique number.

ASSESSING SKILLS

Now that you have your subprojects and you've assigned deliverables to each, it's time to reassess the composition of your team, to make sure you have the right people on the team to accomplish the work of the subprojects. If you have a small project and therefore the people on the main project team will actually do the work of creating the deliverables, then you need to assess their skills versus the skills required to do the work. Some questions to ask include the following:

- ✔ Are there any interim deliverables that cannot be produced by a member of the team? If so, what kind of skills will you need to recruit or are these skills that could be outsourced?

- ✔ Are there any subprojects that don't seem a good match for the team member you recruited or that was assigned to you? Is there someone else in the organization who might be a better match to produce the deliverables you'll need for that subproject?

If you're going to complete the project successfully, you need people with the right set of skills to create the deliverables. Now is the time to determine if you need additional help or a different kind of help. There is no shame in someone bowing off a team because he or she is not the best person to get the job done. Quite the opposite. That only demonstrates the person is willing to put the good of the project above his own personal good. Assign each person on the team to one of the subprojects. Write his name under the name of the subproject.

If you have a large project with subproject teams, then it's the responsibility of the subproject leader to assess the skills he or she will need and make any team-member changes that might be necessary to get the best match between the work that needs to get done and the people who can do the work.

ASSESSING STAKEHOLDER REPRESENTATION

In addition to assuring that you have the skills you need to get the job done, you also need to make sure that all the key stakeholders have appropriate representation on the team. Review the list of stakeholders from your stakeholder form in light of the work you've done in planning to further define the scope of the project (see Figure 6.4). Have all the stakeholders been identified? If not, add any newly identified ones to the stakeholder form.

For each stakeholder, determine if he or she is a key stakeholder. Key stakeholders are people or groups that are significantly impacted by the project. They include the following:

✔ The project customer

✔ Major suppliers that provide inputs to the project

✔ Resource area managers that provide resources (usually people and sometimes money, as well) to the project

STAKEHOLDER FORM

Stakeholder Group	Type of Stakeholder	How Affected by the Project?	Key Stakeholder?	Team Status	Team Member Liaison

Figure 6.4 Stakeholder form.

105

✔ Project leaders from projects in which there is a major overlap in scope

✔ Anyone else who is significantly impacted by the project

Check off each stakeholder on your form who qualifies as a key stakeholder.

Now you need to determine what type of representation each stakeholder should have. There are three categories for stakeholder representation:

1. *Regular team membership.* Stakeholders are included on the team as a regular team member, which means they attend all project team meetings and participate fully in the planning and monitoring of the project. This is usually appropriate for key stakeholders.

2. *Ad hoc team membership.* They can be ad hoc members of the team, which means they attend meetings only when their inputs are required. This may apply to stakeholders who are not key stakeholders.

3. *No team membership.* Assign a member of the team to be a liaison to the stakeholder group, to get their inputs on topics and to communicate back to the stakeholder on what is going on in the project. This is called a team member liaison. This applies to stakeholders who don't fit the first two categories.

Some teams are hesitant to include the customer as a regular member of the team. There are several reasons why including the customer is a good idea:

✔ Participation on the team by the customer will ensure his or her buy-in to the team's decisions.

✔ The customer will understand the trade-off decisions that will be made over the course of the project.

106

✔ The customer can provide valuable input about what the needs and requirements are throughout the project.

Ad hoc membership is a good choice if you have a technical expert who you'll need on the team but you don't want that individual to be a regular member. It is also appropriate for key suppliers or even for the customer when category one doesn't make sense.

In large projects with subproject teams, the resource areas usually assign the subproject leaders. That allows the subproject leader access to the resources needed to do the work of his or her subproject, and the resource area then has representation on the team. Subproject leaders must be regular team members. They will be accountable to make sure the deliverables listed next to their subprojects are completed, as required, on time (which we haven't determined yet) and within budget (also not determined). Make sure there is one and only one subproject leader for each subproject. Write that person's name under the name of the subproject.

TEAM MEMBER LIAISONS

Stakeholders are important because they can make or break a project, particularly if a project involves implementing a plan or design of some type. Stakeholders are typically the ones who will have to run the processes or services that you have installed. Resistance to the implementation can mean the death of what you and your team may have spent months putting together. For example, suppose you redesign a business process but don't include the stakeholders for the business process on the team. Once you've completed your redesign, the business process managers are expected to implement the new design, but they did not participate in the redesign process. How receptive do you think they'll be to the changes you are proposing? People typically don't like to change and they particularly don't like other people dictating what changes they need to make. Save yourself a lot of headaches and include the stakeholders in the project. Here again, their participation will pay off in increased understanding, accuracy, ownership, and commitment.

Not every stakeholder can be on the team. That would make the project team too large and cumbersome. When team membership is not necessary, assign a liaison from the team to keep the stakeholder informed about what is going on, and solicit his or her ideas and inputs to bring back to the team. (The team member liaison must be a regular team member.)

Record the team status (regular or ad hoc or none) for each stakeholder on your stakeholder form. If the stakeholder will not be on the team, add the name of the team member liaison to the last column on the form.

MAKING TEAM MEMBERSHIP CHANGES

You should now have a complete list of the regular and ad hoc members of your team. If the list varies from your initial team then you'll need to get an approval from the sponsor and any affected resource managers to make the team assignment changes. It will help if you show them the analysis you've done—the deliverables to be produced, the skills assessment, and the stakeholder form—to help support your request for a change in team assignment.

THE SUBPROJECT TREE DIAGRAM

If you followed the instructions for how to organize your project, you've basically completed the organizational chart for your project, which we call a subproject tree diagram (see Figure 6.5). The subproject tree is a graphical display of how the project is organized (what are the subprojects), what will be delivered by each subproject, and who is accountable for what.

Draw the main trunk of the tree to the left of your subprojects and write the name of the project on it. Then draw a branch for each sub-

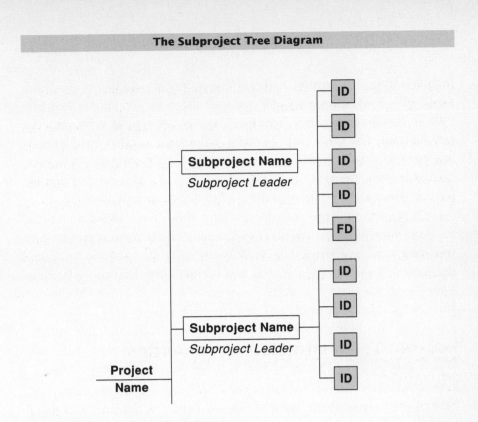

Figure 6.5 Subproject tree diagram.

project. The name of the person accountable for the subproject should be written underneath the subproject branch.

From each subproject branch, draw branches to each of your deliverables (interim or final). Double-check to make sure you haven't missed any deliverables and that no one deliverable shows up in more than one subproject.

Tip: The reason a deliverable should not be in more than one subproject is that the placement of the deliverable indicates who is accountable to make sure the deliverable is produced, and a cardinal rule of accountability is to never have more than one person accountable for a single output or deliverable, even if more than one person will be involved in producing the deliverable.

Your subproject tree should look like an organizational chart turned on its side, and that's exactly what it is—the organizational chart for the project. In addition, it shows the work that will be done by each subproject. Sometimes this is referred to as the work breakdown structure (WBS). However, there is a difference between the typical WBS and your tree diagram: The WBS usually shows all the activities that must be done and not just the deliverables. This makes the WBS detailed and unnecessarily complex. Because the CORE PM method focuses on deliverables, we don't need all the tasks or activities listed in our tree diagram.

However, in larger projects, where there are subproject teams, each subproject leader will want to have his or her team create its own tree diagram (see Figure 6.6). It is appropriate at that time to extend the branches one more level and add the activities that must be completed to create the deliverables. They can also add the name of the person who will be responsible to complete each activity.

Tip: We differentiate between the terms accountability and responsibility. If you are accountable for something, you must make sure it gets done. If you are responsible, you do the task yourself.

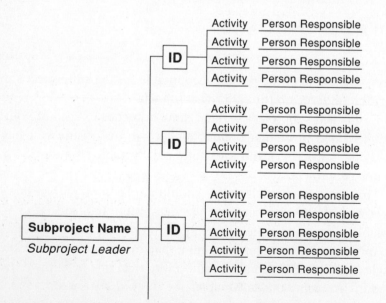

Figure 6.6 Tree diagram for a subproject.

Note: It's important to remember that the subproject tree breakdown does not show the order in which the deliverables will be produced, when they will be produced, or any interdependencies with other deliverables. We'll get to that later when we create the deliverables schedule.

EMPOWERMENT OF THE TEAM

Organizing the project and assigning accountability for each subproject and each deliverable is one of the activities that will help you to empower the team. The benefit of empowerment is that you get the work done without having to monitor every detail of what each person is doing. The requirement of empowerment is that you have to be willing to let go of control. However, successful empowerment does not involve just handing someone a deliverable to produce and then hoping they get it done properly. Here are some conditions necessary for successful empowerment of team members:

- ✔ Team members participate in the planning and monitoring of the project.
- ✔ Everyone on the team understands the big picture of the project—why it is being done, its purpose.
- ✔ Everyone on the team understands the interdependencies of the project—how all the pieces fit together. (We'll get to this when we do the deliverables schedule.)
- ✔ The project focuses on deliverables, and accountability is assigned for each deliverable. This allows team members the freedom to choose the best way to create the deliverables.
- ✔ There is regular status reporting by team members to the team.
- ✔ The team has the resources required to get the job done. This includes the time, money, and people. (We'll address these issues as we work through resource planning in later chapters.)

111

Focusing on deliverables instead of activities keeps the project team at the appropriate level of detail and keeps them from micro-managing individual project member or subproject leaders. There are some other benefits of working with deliverables:

✔ Deliverables are passed from one person to another. This is called a hand-off. Coordination in a project is primarily required when there is a hand-off, particularly between one subproject and another. Deliverables help you to identify these hand-offs.

✔ Deliverables have a due date and so you know if they are completed on time.

✔ You can assign a cost to a deliverable.

✔ You can assign customer acceptance criteria to critical interim deliverables.

These criteria are set by the next customer of the deliverable, the next person in the input/output chain we discussed earlier. The internal customer for a deliverable is usually one of the other members of the team, and that internal customer would define his or her requirements for the interim deliverable and the criteria for acceptance. Setting internal customer acceptance criteria will not only help to ensure that the quality of the final deliverable stays on track, but it will also help the team to avoid rework.

CONTENT AND PROCESS CHECK

Before moving on to risk assessment, do a quick content and process check to make sure you haven't missed anything.

❑ Have you identified someone to provide each of the key skills needed to create the deliverables?

❑ Have all of the key stakeholders been identified?

❏ Does each stakeholder have representation on the team, either as a regular or ad hoc member, or by having a team-member liaison?

❏ Did the team participate in breaking the project down into subprojects?

❏ Have you kept the main project team to a manageable size—less than ten team members?

❏ Did you include a subproject for project management?

❏ Are each of the project's interim and final deliverables included in only one of the subprojects?

❏ Are all the subproject interim deliverables listed in the subproject tree?

❏ Has accountability been assigned for each subproject and each subproject deliverable?

❏ Has each team member accepted the accountability assigned to him or her?

THE PROJECT PLAN DOCUMENT

Now you're ready to add the project organization information to the Project Plan. You'll want to include the subproject tree in the plan. This will allow everyone to see at a glance how your project is organized (the subprojects), who is accountable for what, and what each subproject will produce (the interim deliverables).

Also include the stakeholder form. This allows reviewers of the plan to check the table to make sure you haven't missed any stakeholders and that the appropriate level of team membership has been granted to each stakeholder.

You have now completed the scope and organization parts of the project plan. You're ready to explore potential problems the project might run into when it's executed, and you can decide how to avoid these problems from occurring. This is called risk assessment.

Chapter

Assessing Risk

Have you ever had unexpected events cause your best-laid plans to go astray? For example, let's say it's the day of the product launch dinner/dance. The caterer is arriving with the food, and you notice that there is only enough food for 100 people and you're having 200. Or, it begins to rain and you're having the reception on the lawn and no one thought to order a tent. These risks might have been avoided and you would have had a much smoother, more enjoyable event if you had taken the time to figure out how to execute the project with as little disruption as possible. The planning activity that helps you avoid unnecessary problems is called risk assessment.

A risk is a problem that might occur. The goal in assessing risk is to prevent potential problems from turning into real problems. How could you have avoided the catering problem cited above? Well, you could have checked the references for the caterer to make sure he or she was reliable. You could have checked in with him the night before to make sure he was prepared for the big day. What about the potential rain? How would risk assessment help you with something as uncontrollable as the weather? Well, you could have reserved a tent and then watched the weather forecast to see if you'd need it. You could have opted to move the reception inside. These are examples of

114

risk responses—ways in which to prevent or avoid the risks that are identified.

The reason you assess risk is to help you execute your project with as few of the following problems as possible:

✔ Delay

✔ Rework

✔ Added cost

✔ Headaches and ulcers

TYPES OF RISKS

There are three types of risk (see Table 7.1.):

Scope risk is any potential problem that could prevent you from producing a quality final deliverable, that is, one that meets the customer's acceptance criteria. Scope risk is sometimes known as technical risk, and it includes potential technology or technical capability problems. In the dinner/dance example, the potential problem of having food for 100 instead of 200 would be a scope risk; because if half of our attendees go hungry, it's not likely they will be satisfied with the event.

The second type of risk, schedule risk, is the risk of not producing the final deliverable on time. Some scope or technical risks are also

TABLE 7.1 Types of Risk	
Risk Type	*Description*
Scope risk	The risk of not being able to meet the customer's acceptance criteria. Also known as technical risk.
Schedule risk	The risk of not being able to meet the schedule deadlines, particularly the deadline for the final deliverable.
Cost risk	The risk of exceeding the spending limit.

schedule risks. For example, if you are going to use new technology that you're not familiar with, you might not be successful in implementing that new technology properly (scope risk), and it might take you longer to learn the new technology than you thought (schedule risk).

Finally there is cost risk or the risk of not meeting the budget. An example of a cost risk would be that the people at the dinner/dance would drink more than you projected and your refreshment bill would go over budget.

In the risk assessment process we'll discuss shortly, you'll identify all three types of risks at the same time, and you don't have to worry about which category they belong to. But, it's helpful to know the difference between the types so you can make sure you've identified potential problems in all three categories.

There are three stages in our basic risk assessment process: identify the risks, analyzing them, and then develop countermeasures for them (ways to avoid them from occurring). You'll work through these three stages during your risk assessment meeting.

RISK ASSESSMENT MEETING

It's important to have the right people at your risk assessment meeting. Don't just invite members of the team. Invite everyone who might help you identify or discover potential problems. Table 7.2 indicates the people or groups that should be invited to your risk identification meeting:

People outside the team add value to the risk assessment process by:

- ✔ Adding another source of ideas.
- ✔ Leveraging a scarce resource, especially someone needed by the team, but who can't be a team member.
- ✔ Obtaining commitment and buy-in to the solutions and countermeasures generated.

TABLE 7.2 Risk Assessment Invitees	
Risk Type	*Description*
Project team & leader	Team members can help to identify risks and because they participate in the process, they will take ownership of the work that will need to be done to reduce or prevent the risks from occurring.
Sponsor & in the customer	The sponsor and customer have a large stake project. If they help to identify risks, they'll feel more comfortable that everything possible is being done to prevent problems from occurring.
Other stakeholders	Other stakeholders include the resource or functional managers, key suppliers, and anyone else affected by the project. These people have an interest in the project and will contribute ideas and end up as supporters if you include them in the meeting.
Naysayers	These are people who are potentially negative about your project. By inviting them to the meeting, you gain their ideas about what could go wrong and potentially gain their commitment to the project.
Technical experts	Invite people who know something about the technical aspects of your project. They can help to identify potential technical problems.
People with similar project experience (projects involved in similar technology or serving the same customers, and so on.)	Invite people who have worked on similar projects in the past. Their experiences will be helpful, particularly if you haven't captured historical data from those projects.

✔ Getting their concerns on the table so they can be addressed head on.

✔ Benefiting from other people's experiences.

✔ Moving them from complaining to being a part of the solution.

✔ Raising awareness of your project's needs and risks.

✔ Increasing stakeholders' understanding of project issues and challenges.

✔ Developing buy-in and commitment to the solution.

✔ Turning detractors into supporters!

Before you assemble the group, reserve a large enough room so that everyone can sit comfortably but still move around easily, because most of the work will be done using self-stick notes on flip-chart or banner paper taped to the wall. Stock up on self-stick notes and markers and you're ready to begin.

STAGE ONE—IDENTIFYING RISKS

The first stage, identifying risks, begins with brainstorming. Ask the group to brainstorm all the things that could go wrong with the project. Give each team member a set of self-stick notes and a marker and ask them to record the risks as they identify them. Tape a piece of banner paper to the wall and let people call out the risks, write them down, and then walk up to the paper and slap the self-stick note on the wall, all at the same time. Don't take turns. Everyone should brainstorm together. This brainstorming method is called Write it! Say it! Slap it!™ and it's another example of a team-based tool that uses all three learning styles: visual (self-stick notes), auditory (say it!) and kinesthetic (slap it!). (See Chapter 3, principle 4 for more information on learning styles.)

When brainstorming, it's important to keep these simple rules in mind:

✔ All ideas are good ideas.

✔ Make sure each idea is complete; do not use one word ideas because you'll forget later what they meant.

✔ Make sure each idea is recorded and posted on paper. It's best to use self-stick notes that are then posted on flip-chart or banner paper. They can be moved around easily and everyone in the brainstorming session can view the ideas.

✔ Duplicates are okay. (Sometimes an idea appears to be a duplicate but during the discussion afterwards you discover it's actually a different idea.)

✔ Go for quantity, not quality.

✔ Think outside the box—get crazy.

✔ No judgment.

✔ Don't stop and discuss.

✔ Keep the momentum going.

When the group seems to have exhausted its ideas, ask them for ten more. That will help the group push the envelope a little. Next, ask the group to identify any assumptions they hold, which if proved not to be true, would create a problem for the project. For example, an assumption about our dinner/dance is that the 50-mile drive from the office to Magnolia Plantation will not be a deterrent to attendance. Then ask yourself, what if the assumption weren't true? Key invited guests might not come and the whole point of having the celebration is to thank people for the work they did on the development and launch of the new product. Therefore, the risk of no-shows due to distance should be included as a risk for our project.

Record the group's assumptions on a sheet of paper. Then convert these assumptions to risks by asking what would happen if each assumption were not true and, as a result, would cause a problem for the project. Write the problem or the risk on a self-stick note and include it with the other brainstormed risks.

STAGE TWO—ANALYZING RISKS

Once you have identified all the possible things that could go wrong during the project, it's time to define how likely it is that each of those potential problems might occur and, if they were to do so, the impact or damage that would be caused by the occurrence. The chance that something might occur is called the risk probability. The damage that would incur is called the risk impact.

Risk Probability

First, rate the probability of occurrence as zero, low, medium, or high. (See Table 7.3.)

When you have consensus on the probability rating, write it in the lower left-hand corner of the self-stick note. Zero-probability risks are events we know will not occur. Move these to the side under the zero-risk heading.

Risk Impact

Next, ask the group to rate the impact of each of the brainstormed risks. Write the rating—zero, low, medium or high—on the bottom right-hand side of the self-stick note. For example, the risk impact of

TABLE 7.3 Risk-Probability Ratings	
Probability Rating	Meaning
Zero	There is no chance that this risk will occur
Low (L)	The probability that this event will occur is between 1 and 40%
Medium (M)	The probability that this event will occur is between 41 and 70%
High (H)	The probability that this event will occur is between 71 and 99%

not having enough food to feed all the guests is high, but the probability of not having enough food is low. Zero-impact risks are events that have no impact on the project. Move these to the side under the zero-risk heading. (See Table 7.4.)

RISK PI MATRIX

After you've rated each risk, it's helpful to organize them so you can see which are the worst risks. We do this by placing each risk into a risk analysis matrix, also known as a Probability/Impact matrix or PI matrix for short. Draw a nine-square grid on banner paper and label the vertical or *y*-axis as probability and the horizontal or *x*-axis as impact. Fill in the low, medium, or high ratings on the axes as shown in Figure 7.1.

Note that some boxes are labeled "low." This means that risks that fall into those squares on the matrix are low risks. The label in the squares takes into account both probability and impact. Risks that fall into the squares marked "medium" are medium risks. You'll note that one of the boxes marked "medium" corresponds to risks with low

TABLE 7.4 Risk Impact Ratings	
Probability Rating	*Meaning*
Zero	There is no impact if this risk should occur; therefore, it's not truly a risk
Low	The impact on the project is minor, but would be noticed by the customer or sponsor
Medium	The impact to the project is not insignificant and would cause the team to miss the CAC, the deadlines, or overspend the budget
High	The impact is significant and would jeopardize or kill the project

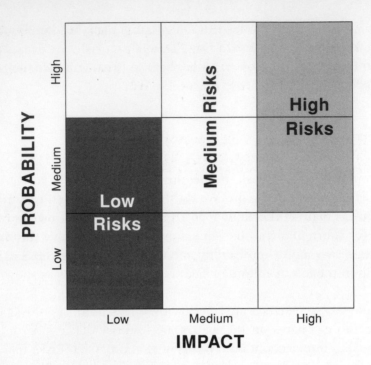

Figure 7.1 PI matrix diagram.

probability and high impact, but the overall rating for this risk would be medium.

Number all the risks on the grid consecutively, starting at the top right and working down to the bottom left. The order isn't particularly important; just assign a unique number to each risk. It will make it easier to keep track of them later.

ASSESSING OVERALL RISK

Now it's time to step back and look at the distribution of the risks on the grid and ask the team, "How risky is this project overall?" Is it highly risky? Medium? Low? Do your risks cluster in the upper right-hand side of the grid? If so, you've got a high-risk project. Do they cluster in the bottom left? Then it's a low-risk project. In the middle or evenly dispersed? Medium risk (see Figure 7.2).

The goal for most projects is low risk, so what you'll do next is to see what can be done to lower the level of risk.

STAGE THREE—DEVELOP AND ANALYZE COUNTERMEASURES

For each risk in the medium or high sections of the matrix, brainstorm ways to prevent the risk from occurring or reduce the probability and/or impact of the risk. For example, ideas to reduce the risk of not having enough food include the following: go over the final

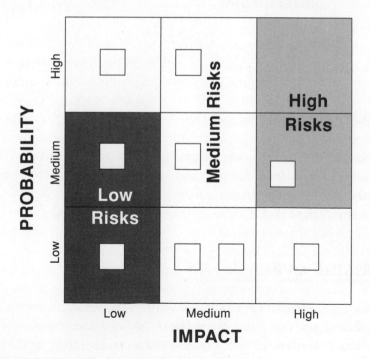

Figure 7.2 PI matrix for a medium-risk project.

123

arrangements with the caterer 48 hours ahead of time (which reduces the probability), have a buffet (reduces the impact), order more food than you need (reduces the probability), have extra drinks (reduces impact). Not all of these are good ideas, but you're just brainstorming at this point.

Write each countermeasure idea on a self-stick note and attach it to the risk self-stick note. Write the number of the risk on the countermeasure self-stick note. Work through each risk, brainstorming potential countermeasures. If a single countermeasure addresses more than one risk, write the risk numbers on the note and attach it to one of the risks.

Once you've finished the brainstorming process, you'll need to choose which countermeasures to include in your project plan. Obviously, the ones that are free—that don't add time to the schedule or costs to the budget—should be added first. Next, add any countermeasures that address multiple risks and that are good ideas. Then add countermeasures that reduce the risk from a high or medium level to a low level.

Tip: Make sure the countermeasures you choose don't end up costing more money or time than the risk you're trying to lower. If this is the case, you're better off with the problem than paying for the solution.

Choose countermeasures that are consistent with the project priorities set down in the charter. The choices were scope, schedule, or budget. If the top priority was schedule, don't add countermeasures that will add time to your schedule. If your top priority was cost, then obviously adding costs will not be your first option, although it may be one you need to propose in order to lower the risk.

As you select a countermeasure, assign someone on the team to be accountable for the countermeasure. Write that person's name on the countermeasure self-stick note.

Then, reassess the impact and probability ratings for the risk(s) that the countermeasure will affect, and write the new impact and probability ratings above the old ones on the risk self-stick note. (Use a red marker so you can differentiate the old ratings from the new ones.) Then, transfer the risk self-stick note to the square on the grid that corresponds to the new probability and impact ratings (see Figure 7.3).

124

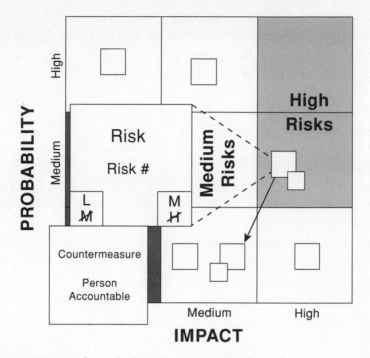

Figure 7.3 Transfer risks based on new ratings.

REASSESSING OVERALL RISK

Once you have selected the countermeasures, revised your probability and impact ratings, and moved the self-stick notes, you need to step back and reassess the overall risk of the project. Is the project still of a high or medium risk? If so, you'll need to discuss the situation with your sponsor to find out what he or she wants you to do about the remaining risks. Maybe a medium or high risk project is acceptable to him or her. Or, maybe the sponsor will agree that you can spend more time or money, or change the project scope in order to reduce the risk. These are options he or she will need to decide, in consultation with the customer.

CONTENT AND PROCESS CHECK

Before you wrap-up your risk assessment, make sure you haven't missed anything.

- ❏ Did you invite technical experts, stakeholders, naysayers, and team members to the risk assessment meeting?
- ❏ Were all risks identified? Did you have outsiders in your risk assessment to make sure you didn't miss anything?
- ❏ Did you eliminate those risks that had a zero impact or probability?
- ❏ Did you brainstorm all possible countermeasures including some that sounded crazy?
- ❏ Were the countermeasures chosen based on the project's priorities?
- ❏ Did you assign someone to be accountable for each countermeasure?
- ❏ Is your overall project risk low and, if not, have you gotten permission from your sponsor to spend additional resources or reduce the scope so that you can lower the risk? Or, has the sponsor agreed to accept a higher level of risk?

PROJECT PLAN DOCUMENT

Your final step is to document the information you've gathered. A simple form is the best way to capture the work you have done with the risk assessment group. (See Figure 7.4.)

Write the name of the project and the name of the project leader. Then list the original risk rating for the project before you developed the countermeasures. Next, list the final risk rating for the project, with the countermeasures.

In the body of the table, write the risk number, the name of the

RISK ASSESSMENT FORM

Project Name: _____   Original Risk Rating: _____

Project Leader: _____   Final Risk Rating: _____

Risk #	Risk	P rating	I rating	Countermeasures	Counter-measures Included?	Person accountable	New P rating	New I rating

Figure 7.4 Risk assessment form.

risk, the original probability and impact ratings. List all of the counter-measures that were brainstormed for the risk, including those you did not include. Next, place a check mark after those you will use and then write the name of the person who is accountable to make sure the countermeasure gets done. Finally, record the new probability and impact ratings for the risk, based on implementing the countermeasure.

Congratulations. You're done with your risk assessment.

Chapter 8

Developing a Schedule

A schedule tells you what will be done, by when. Most projects need two different types of schedules: a milestone schedule and a deliverables schedule. A milestone schedule is the 10,000 foot view of the project schedule. It shows the 10 to 12 major accomplishments for the project, and the dates those accomplishments will be completed. The deliverables schedule is the 100 foot view. It shows every deliverable that will be produced, the date it will be produced, and the interdependencies between the deliverables.

The purpose of the milestone schedule is to highlight the major elements of the schedule and communicate those to the stakeholders.

The deliverables schedule serves a number of purposes. It

✔ Shows the delivery date for each deliverable and which sub-project will produce the deliverable.

✔ Maps the interdependencies between the deliverables.

✔ Shows the milestone dates.

✔ Provides a means of monitoring the progress of deliverables when you get into the execution phase of the project.

✔ Shows the technical-process flow from the first deliverable to the last.

The technical-process flow is the set of steps (deliverables) that are required to produce the final deliverable. This process is a series of hand-offs of interim deliverables from one person to the next (the input/output chain discussed earlier). The deliverables schedule is basically a process-flow diagram showing when each deliverable is created and who will receive the deliverable to create the next deliverable in the chain. Because the flow of work with interdependencies is depicted in the deliverables schedule, with due dates for each deliverable, the deliverables schedule is one of the most important elements of your project plan.

Note: If you think that the people on your team already know the technical-process flow, think again. Chances are that mapping the flow during the deliverables schedule exercise will be a real eye-opener for some of them and even the very experienced folks are often surprised to see how their work fits into the big picture.

The first step to creating a milestone and deliverables schedule is to pick your milestone events.

PICKING THE MILESTONE EVENTS

The first three milestone events you'll need to include are the phase gates. These represent the major accomplishments in the project management process. The first phase gate, the charter document, is not included as a milestone because it was completed before you started the planning phase. The other phase gates—the completion of the project plan (that signals the end of the planning phase), the delivery of the final deliverable to the customer (that signals the end of the execution phase), and the completion of the close-out report (the end of the close-out phase)—should be on the milestone schedule.

In addition, you'll want to add six to ten milestone dates during the execution phase of the project. If you have stage gates, use these. (Stage gates are major points of accomplishment in the technical process. These are usually set by the organization as go/no go decision points.) Otherwise, you'll need to choose six to ten major deliverables that each represent major segments of work completed. The deliverables chosen can be produced by either the main project or one of the subprojects, just so long as it's an important deliverable for the project. If you were given a deadline date by the sponsor or customer, then that event or deliverable should be a milestone event, because, by assigning it as a deadline, the sponsor or customer signals that they consider this to be important, and the milestone schedule reflects the most important deliverables. When you're thinking about which milestones to include, consider that this is the schedule for people outside the team. Ask yourself, "What accomplishments would the sponsor, customer, and other key stakeholders consider to be significant?"

Try to choose milestones that span the execution phase of the project. If your milestones are all bunched up at the beginning or the end of execution, your stakeholders will not be able to tell if your project is on time or not. This creates insecurity that can lead to meddling, which most people would rather avoid. Spreading out the milestones (see Figure 8.1) provides the stakeholders assurance throughout the project that you are managing just fine, thank you very much, and they will have less reason to panic and attempt to intervene.

After you've chosen the milestone events, write the name of each one in the center of a self-stick note. If the sponsor or customer gave you a deadline for the milestone (like the deadline for the final deliverable), write that deadline in red in the bottom right corner. (You'll use

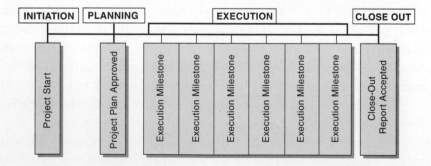

Figure 8.1 Space the milestones across the project timeline.

these self-stick notes when you create the deliverables schedule, which you'll do next.) If you were not given a deadline date, then leave that space blank.

Next, team members will need to prepare for the deliverables-schedule meeting. In preparation for this meeting, each team member should prepare self-stick notes for his or her deliverables, including any countermeasures that were assigned to them during the risk assessment meeting. Then they should estimate how much time will be required to produce each of their deliverables or countermeasures.

ESTIMATING STAFF EFFORT FOR DELIVERABLES

The actual working time in hours or weeks that is required to produce a deliverable is called staff-effort time or just staff effort. So, for example, in the dinner/dance project, the amount of time it would take to create a proposed attendee list would be the staff-effort time for that deliverable. Let's suppose the staff effort estimated is 12 hours or one-and-a-half days. When you estimate staff effort for a deliverable, you're estimating the actual time required to create that deliverable. In other words, it's not the number of days over which you need to spread the effort because you're doing ten other things or waiting for information from other people; it's the actual time you will devote to working on the deliverable.

Most people don't work on projects full time, and, therefore, the calendar time that will be required to create a deliverable will be longer than the staff-effort time. If, for example, you have a regular job and are working on two other projects as well, you might figure that you can devote a portion, say 20 percent, of your time to produce your deliverable. The calendar time for the deliverable or duration required to create the invitee list would be 7.5 days (12 hours or 1.5 days divided by 20 percent = 7.5 days to complete the deliverable).

Unless you're working on a deliverable 100 percent of your time and you don't have to wait to get information from anyone, the duration for a deliverable will always be longer than the staff-effort time.

131

The more projects and other work you have to do, the longer the duration for a deliverable.

Note: Duration should be expressed as the number of work days, calendar weeks, or calendar months required to complete the deliverable. Five work days is typically the equivalent of one calendar week.

Duration should be estimated by the person who is responsible to complete the deliverable, based on his or her experience, the experience of others, and any historical data available from prior projects. If you have a large project with subprojects, each subproject leader should ask their team members to estimate durations for their deliverables. As with any estimate, it's always just that—their best guesses. When you are estimating duration for an individual deliverable, don't add in a fudge factor for unexpected problems, always known as Murphy's Law. This fudge factor is called contingency, and it's better to add a lump of contingency at the end of the project, rather than adding it to each deliverable. There are two principal reasons for adding contingency to the end of the schedule:

1. You end up with more contingency than you need when every deliverable includes a fudge factor. Although you know that Murphy's Law will strike but you don't know where or when, by adding it everywhere, you end up with more than you need.

2. People squander the contingency time when it's included in their deliverable durations. Because people are so busy, they tend not to start the deliverable on the start date, but, instead, wait until the last minute based on the due date. If the contingency is included in the deliverable and you start late, you've already used the contingency as a result of starting late. Now, if Murphy's Law hits, you're going to be late, and you have no contingency left to make up for problems that arise. It's better to estimate the normal time it would take to produce the deliverable and then have a pool of time at the end of the schedule that can be reallocated to an individual when problems hit.

Ask team members to record the staff-effort time and duration on the bottom of each deliverable self-stick note. Write the deliverable name and number (from the subproject tree) in the center of the note (see Figure 8.2).

Tip: Assign each subproject a different colored self-stick note. This will help to visually differentiate the deliverables when you assemble the schedule.

After staff effort and duration are estimated, you're ready to hold the deliverables schedule meeting.

CREATING THE SCHEDULE GRID

To prepare for the deliverables-schedule meeting, reserve a large room with plenty of wall space. Tape banner paper, at least 10 feet in length, to the wall. Draw a large grid and, along the bottom of the grid, record the timeline for the project (divided into weeks, months, quarters, depending on the length of the project).

Along the left-hand side of the grid write the names of the subprojects. If you have a long schedule, you might want to write the subproject names on the right side of the grid as well. Draw horizontal lines (swim lanes) between each subproject (see Figure 8.3).

Tip: Leave enough room between each subproject for at least two rows of self-stick notes.

Place each milestone self-stick note on the timeline (along the

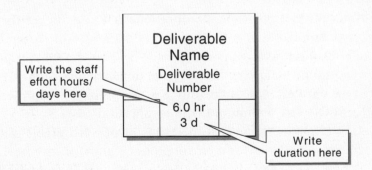

Deliverable Name

Write the staff effort hours/ days here

Deliverable Number

6.0 hr

3 d

Write duration here

Figure 8.2 Deliverables self-stick note.

133

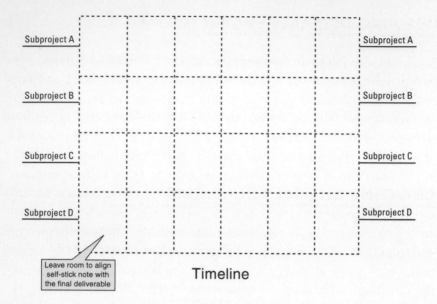

Figure 8.3 Schedule grid.

horizontal axis at the bottom) at the approximate point at which you think that milestone will be completed. If you have a deadline date for the milestone, write the deadline date in red on the bottom of the self-stick note and place the milestone event at the deadline date. If you know why the deadline was set, add a self-stick note with the explanation to the milestone.

Note: When a milestone deadline date is written in red then you know it's a date that was given to you by the sponsor or customer and cannot be changed without permission. When you determine dates for your nondeadline milestones, write them in pencil, indicating that you created the date and, therefore, until the project plan is approved, you can change the date if you want without approval.

Ask each team member to place his or her deliverable self-stick notes in the swim lane (for their subproject), lining them up with the timelines based on their approximation of when the deliverables would be completed. Don't write any dates on the notes yet.

DEFINING INTERDEPENDENCIES

Before you can define the delivery dates, you first need to define the interdependencies between the deliverables—the predecessors and successors. A predecessor is a deliverable that serves as an input to the next deliverable or a deliverable that the next deliverable is dependent on in some way. For example, for our dinner/dance project, because the deliverable "printed invitations" must be completed before the deliverable "mailed invitations" can be started, there is an interdependency between these two deliverables, and "printed invitations" is a predecessor to "mailed invitations." "Mailed invitations," which depends on "printed invitations" is the successor. You can have more than one predecessor or successor for a deliverable (see Figure 8.4).

MAPPING THE INTERDEPENDENCIES

To define the delivery dates for a deliverable, you'll first need to identify predecessors for the deliverables you want to schedule. Start with the self-stick notes on the far left; these are the deliverables that must be

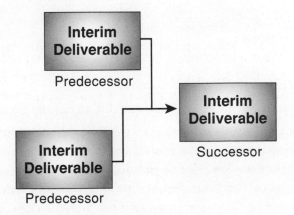

Figure 8.4 Predecessors and successors.

135

created first. For each deliverable, ask if there are any predecessors that must be completed before the deliverable in question can be started. When you find a deliverable that does not have any predecessors, calculate the delivery date for that deliverable as follows:

- ✔ Write the date you plan to start creating the deliverable in the lower left-hand corner of the self-stick note. This is the start date. (It's best to write it in pencil so that you can change it if you need to while you complete the scheduling exercise.)
- ✔ Add the duration to the start date. (The duration should already be recorded in the bottom, middle part of the self-stick note.) The duration should be expressed in working days, weeks, or months. The start date plus the duration is the delivery date.
- ✔ Write the delivery date, in pencil, in the lower right-hand corner

After you have scheduled the deliverables that don't have predecessors, move on to the deliverables that depend solely on those initial deliverables. Calculate the start date and delivery date for each successor. The start date is usually the day following the latest delivery date of a predecessor. For deliverables that have more than one predecessor, use the latest predecessor delivery date to calculate the start date for the successor deliverable (see Figure 8.5).

Continue to work from one deliverable to the next as you:

- ✔ Identify all the predecessors.
- ✔ Identify the latest delivery date for any of the predecessors.
- ✔ Set the start date for the next deliverable. If possible, the start date should be the day after the latest delivery date of the latest predecessor. Check personal commitments, such as other projects, trips, and so on for interferences before setting a start date.

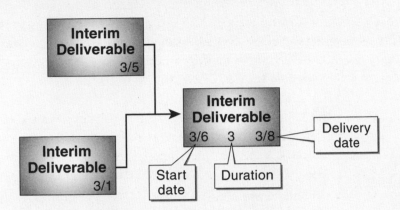

Figure 8.5 Calculating delivery dates.

✔ Add the duration to the start date—this is the delivery date.

✔ Align the self-stick note with the delivery date.

✔ Record the delivery date in the bottom right-hand corner of the self-stick note.

✔ Draw arrows from the predecessor to the successor(s).

After you've scheduled all the deliverables, step back and review the schedule (see Figure 8.6). Look for hanging deliverables that don't have any successors. When a deliverable is not handed off to a customer, then something is wrong: You either don't need that deliverable or it's missing a successor in the process flow.

Record dates of completion for any milestones that do not have deadlines associated with them. If there are milestone deadlines that cannot be met, you'll need to:

✔ Ask the sponsor if there is any leeway in the milestone deadline.

✔ If the deadline cannot be changed, you'll need to revise the schedule. (We'll discuss that in a minute.)

137

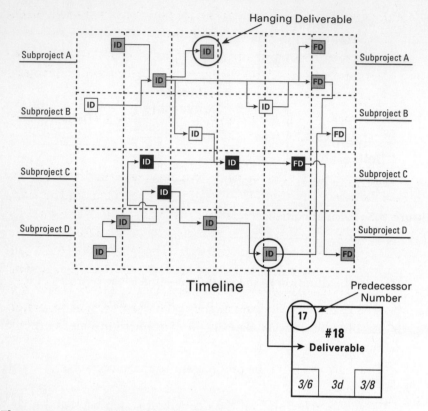

Figure 8.6 The deliverables schedule.

THE BENEFITS OF THE MANUAL METHOD

Creating a schedule with banner paper and self-stick notes has a number of advantages over having the project leader sit down in front of his or her computer and create a schedule using a software program:

✔ Everyone on the team participates in creating the schedule.

✔ Scheduling conflicts between team members can be immediately resolved.

✔ Everyone on the team understands whom he or she will be depending on and who depends on them.

✔ Team members know their own schedules and can adjust the start and delivery dates for their deliverables to best integrate with any other commitments they have.

✔ Everyone on the team understands the big picture and how their pieces fit into the whole.

However, there is one downside to using a self-stick note process to create the schedule: The self-stick notes don't stretch, and so every deliverable appears visually to be of the same duration. This downside is easily rectified if your schedule has been drawn to scale. To see the duration for each deliverable, you can draw a rectangle around the self-stick note that begins at the start date and ends at the delivery date. This converts your schedule to a Gantt chart (see Figure 8.7). Use colored markers to draw the rectangles and try to draw them as accurately as possible.

SLACK TIME

After you've drawn the Gantt chart, you'll notice that some pairs of deliverables will have no space between them. For other pairs there will be a space. This space is called slack time. Slack time is extra time between the delivery date of one deliverable and the start date of the next. This usually happens when there are multiple predecessors for a deliverable and the successor cannot start until the last predecessor is complete, resulting in slack time between the successor and one or more predecessors (see Figure 8.8).

Slack in the schedule means that if the predecessor deliverable (with slack in front of it) is delayed for less time or equal time than the slack time, the successor can still start on time. When there is no slack, a delay in the delivery of the prior deliverable will cause a delay in the start of the successor deliverable.

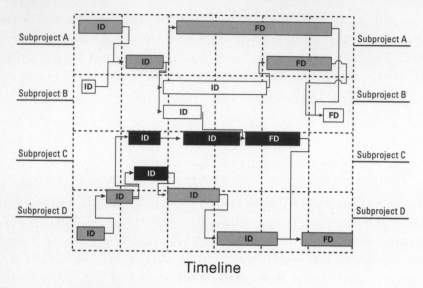

Figure 8.7 The Gantt chart.

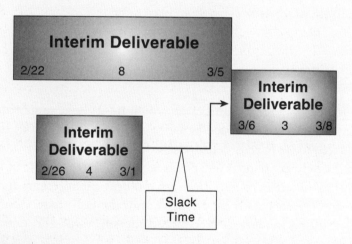

Figure 8.8 Slack time.

For each pair of predecessor/successor deliverables, mark those with a circle that have no slack. If your schedule is not drawn to scale, you can identify the deliverables without slack by reviewing each pair of predecessor/successor relationships and circling those in which there is no time between the completion of the predecessor and the start of the successor.

IDENTIFYING THE CRITICAL PATH

The path through the schedule that has no slack time is called the critical path. The critical path is the longest path through the schedule and it determines the delivery date of the final deliverable. If any deliverable on the critical path is late, then the final deliverable will be late. Because there is no slack along the critical path, the project cannot be done more quickly unless you somehow shorten the critical path.

If you need to shorten the schedule, you'll need to first identify the critical path. If your deliverables schedule is not too complex, you'll be able to connect the circles you drew where there was no slack, and trace the critical path through the schedule (see Figure 8.9). It's a bit like following a maze.

However, if your schedule is complicated, if there are too many deliverables to identify the critical path visually, you'll need to use a computer scheduling program to help. Almost every project management scheduling program will identify the critical path for you. Enter the dates from your deliverables schedule into the software program. You'll need the deliverable name (it's usually called a task in the software), the duration, the start and delivery date, and the predecessors. (Most computer programs will actually calculate the start and delivery dates for you if you have the duration and predecessors, so try entering just the duration and predecessors and see if you get the same start and delivery dates that you generated in the scheduling meeting.) After your deliverables information has been entered, the critical path can be highlighted on the schedule.

141

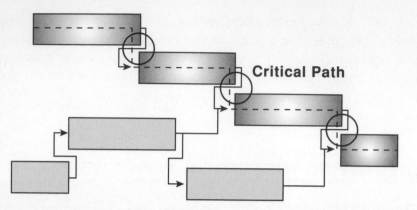

Figure 8.9 Identifying the critical path.

ADDING CONTINGENCY TIME

The problem with all project planning is that you cannot foresee or totally control the future. If you could, projects would be easy. But you can't, so all you can do is project into the future with greater or lesser accuracy. The more knowledgeable you are about the durations of your deliverables and the risks associated with your schedule, the more accurate your schedule will be.

In addition, our ability to predict the future diminishes as we try to project further out into the future. Therefore, shorter schedules tend to be more accurate than long ones.

Because there is always uncertainty when you project into the future or attempt to estimate durations, you should add some contingency to the end of the schedule to cover the uncertainties. Contingency is like an insurance policy. You may not need it, but it's better to have it so that, when Murphy's Law hits, you have a savings account of time to help protect your deadline date.

There is no magic formula for how much contingency you'll need. It will depend on these factors:

142

✔ The complexity of the project. The more complex the project, the more contingency you'll probably need.

✔ The amount of risk in the project. The more risk, the more contingency.

✔ The length of the project. Longer projects require more contingency because it gets harder and harder to predict the future.

✔ If you've done this type of project in the past, you'll need less contingency than if this type of project is new to the project team.

✔ The experience of the team. More experienced teams require less contingency because they are better at estimating.

✔ The amount and accuracy of historical data available from similar projects. If you have accurate data, then your estimates will be closer to reality and you'll need less contingency.

✔ The reliability of vendors. The more unreliable, the more contingency you'll need.

✔ Degree you must share resources with other projects. This creates greater uncertainty in the duration estimates and increases the risk that team members will be pulled off your project to work on other projects.

How much contingency is enough? That's something you'll also have to guess. Until you have good historical data, you're better off adding more than you think you need.

SHORTENING THE SCHEDULE

If your schedule, with contingency, does not allow you to meet your deadline dates, then you'll need to look at shortening it. This does not mean chopping off the contingency. That tactic will only ensure that you will be late, because you will have eliminated time to cover Murphy's Law and Murphy will undoubtedly strike at some point in your project. Here are some questions to ask as you evaluate ways in which you can take time out of the schedule:

✔ Is there a safety cushion built into each duration estimate? Can it be moved from the duration estimate to the end of the schedule? You'll need less total contingency time if it's at the end than embedded in each deliverable.

✔ Can deliverables, which are being created in sequence, be produced in parallel instead?

✔ Can parts of a deliverable be started before the predecessor is complete?

✔ Can you add people or other resources to shorten the duration of a deliverable?

✔ Can reviews be performed by telephone or video conference instead of in person or by mail? (Reviews take time so shortening the length of a review that's on the critical path will shorten the schedule.)

✔ If you have to order equipment, can the order be placed in advance to reserve a spot in the vendor's shop?

✔ Can delivery times be reduced by using an overnight courier or premium shipping?

✔ Can the sponsor help to remove other commitments for a key resource so that he or she can complete their deliverable sooner?

Don't be afraid to ask the sponsor for help or ideas. Take the deliverables schedule to him or her and see where he or she thinks you could find time in the schedule. Beware, however, of just arbitrarily shortening the duration of a deliverable. You end up creating an unrealistic schedule that can't be met and you'll miss your deadlines anyway.

OPTIONS FOR SCHEDULING

What happens if you just can't meet the deadline date? If your project priorities indicate that schedule is more important than costs, you might be able to buy time. You can do this by adding resources to the schedule, such as outside consulting help. If the schedule is more important than scope, then reducing scope may be an option. Brainstorm a couple of different options for narrowing the scope (assuming you must meet the deadline and cost limits), and present these options to the sponsor and customer. That allows them to make a choice about how to best spend the resources—time and money—of the project.

Once you have the deadline versus cost versus scope issue resolved, you can finalize both schedules. Review your milestones and set the milestone dates, based on the dates in your deliverables schedule. Record the start and delivery dates for each deliverable in pen. Redraw your interdependency arrows with a marker. Your schedule is now complete. Now it's time to create your project budget.

CONTENT AND PROCESS CHECK

Now is a good time to take stock and review. Here's a quick checklist:

- ❏ Did you include your risk countermeasures in your schedule?
- ❏ Does every deliverable have a successor (the next deliverable in the chain) or is it delivered to the project customer? There should be no hanging deliverables that are not delivered to someone.
- ❏ Is the schedule realistic? Does the team feel that it is achievable?
- ❏ Did you add some contingency time at the end of the schedule instead of including it in each deliverable duration?
- ❏ Does the contingency amount reflect the amount of risk that exists in the schedule?

145

❑ Does the schedule indicate that you will meet the schedule deadline? If not, have you discussed the schedule with your sponsor?

❑ Have you finalized your milestone schedule?

PROJECT PLAN DOCUMENT

You'll want to include your milestone and deliverables schedules in your project plan document. In order to have a reproducible deliverables schedule, you can enter the data into a software scheduling program and then print an 8.5 inch by 11 inch schedule.

Chapter

Developing a Budget

You're almost done with the planning process. You've defined the scope of your project, completed a risk assessment, and created a schedule. You organized the project so you know who will do what and when it will get done. Now it's time to craft a budget for the project and then to assemble the complete project plan.

There are basically two types of costs that are included in a budget: costs that are internal to the organization—such as the costs of people's time, cross-charges between departments—and costs that are external—such as purchases of equipment or services.

STAFF EFFORT COSTS

All projects consume monetary resources, even if no money is spent outside the organization. There are still internal expenses because the people working on the project aren't cost free. The effort that they expend on the project, which is called staff effort, costs the organization money, in salary, benefits, and overhead expenses. The cost of staff effort is the principal internal cost for a project.

Many organizations ignore the cost of people's time, because projects are done for internal customers and the organization absorbs the cost of the project as part of the cost of doing business. The cost of people's time is usually ignored because it's a sunk cost. It's not a good idea to ignore staff-effort costs because management should know the total estimated cost of a project before they give the go-ahead to begin. If they don't know the cost, they may approve a project for which the benefits do not outweigh the costs. However, it's not your decision whether to estimate staff costs; it's up to the sponsor.

Organizations that get paid for doing projects for external customers usually calculate the cost of their staff-effort time because their ability to make a profit on the project depends on getting paid for staff effort. Whether you do projects for internal or external customers, the steps for calculating staff-effort costs are the same. Let's take a look.

STAFF-EFFORT COSTS

Staff-effort costs are the costs associated with work done on the project by employees. To calculate staff-effort costs, you'll need an estimate of the time each person will spend creating his or her deliverables. This staff effort estimate should appear on the self-stick note for the deliverable you used in the deliverables schedule exercise. Just add up the total staff-effort time by person to get the total deliverables staff effort.

Most of the time on a project will usually be spent producing deliverables, but there is also time that must be spent in attending meetings, resolving issues, writing reports, and so on. This is called project management staff effort.

PROJECT MANAGEMENT STAFF EFFORT

Project management (PM) staff effort is the time required to plan and manage the project. Ask each team member to estimate the time he or she will spend on project management tasks, such as completing status reports, attending team meetings, meeting with stakeholders, to get a total PM staff effort estimate for each person or subproject. Add the deliverables and project management staff effort estimates together to get a total staff-effort estimate for each person or subproject.

One of the benefits of doing the staff-effort estimate, even if it's not required, is that it helps the resource managers know just how much time you'll need from their people. When the resource managers sign the project plan document, they commit to providing the resources documented in the plan. This will also enable them to plan for the project needs. At least they know what they are committing to and it will be more difficult for them to withhold resources that they have signed off on.

After you gather the staff-effort time for each person, you'll need the rate per person per hour, day, week, or month. Sometimes the rate differs by job function and sometimes it's a standard rate by department. Get the correct rate from the resource manager or from accounting.

Multiply the rate times the total staff-effort estimate for each person to get a staff-effort cost.

COMPLETING THE COST ESTIMATE

In addition to staff-effort costs, there may be other internal costs that you may need to estimate as well:

✔ Any cross-charges from other departments
✔ Any overhead charges to the project

In addition to internal costs, most projects incur external costs, which are costs for people or things that must be purchased from outside the organization. Even if you don't estimate internal costs, most projects are required to estimate external ones.

Review the list of deliverables and for each deliverable ask, "Is there anything that needs to be purchased, outside the organization, in order to complete this deliverable?" Record each outside purchase and estimate the cost. External costs will include such items as

✔ Equipment to be purchased.

✔ Outside services, such as consulting services.

✔ Supplies.

✔ Travel.

✔ Shipping.

Add together all the external costs to get an external cost total. Then, if you have internal costs, add the two numbers together to get a total. This is your budget or spending estimate. Next, you need to assess the accuracy of your estimate.

ACCURACY OF THE ESTIMATE

Estimates are just that, estimates. Some are more accurate than others, so you need to convey to your sponsor and other stakeholders just how accurate your estimate is. You do that by adding an accuracy rating and a range to the estimate. For example, if you were my sponsor and I told you that my estimate for the dinner/dance was $19,524, how much would you anticipate the dinner/dance to cost? $19,524. By stating that I am going to spend $19,524 it looks like I have created a very accurate estimate, when in fact, it could be just the opposite—a wild guess. On the other hand, it might be a fairly accurate estimate based on historical data. Stakeholders have no way of knowing how accurate our estimate really is unless we provide them with an accuracy rating.

Let's examine some factors that can affect the accuracy of the estimate:

✔ The experience of the people on the team

✔ The number of times you've created similar deliverables in the past

✔ The accuracy of the historical data on staff effort (assuming there is some historical data) and its applicability to your project

✔ The length of the project (the longer the project, the less accurate the estimate)

Based on these factors, rate the accuracy of your estimate as high (H), medium (M), or low (L).

After you rate the accuracy, add a range to the spending estimate—plus or minus a certain amount—that reflects the accuracy of the estimate. What the range says is because of the uncertainty of our estimate, we might be under our estimate and then again we might be over, but we are very sure that our final estimate will fall within the range.

Here are some suggestions for adding ranges to your estimate:

✔ If you have a high accuracy rating, you might want to use a range of +/– 10 percent. (You would subtract 10 percent of the total from the estimate and add 10 percent to the total to get the range.)

✔ A medium accuracy might require a range of +/– 25 percent.

✔ A low accuracy range might need a range of +/– 50 percent or more.

You don't need to stick with these exact range numbers; they are only examples to give you some guidance about how large a range to use.

Getting back to our dinner/dance estimate, my estimate was $19,524 and I have given it a medium accuracy rating. Now, if I add a range to the number, and give you an estimate with a range between $17,500 to $21,500, do you have a better idea of how much money the project might cost? You do. Are our actual expenditures more likely to be within the range than to be $19,524 exactly? Of course.

Expressing your spending estimate as a range will

✔ More accurately communicate the true potential costs of the project.

✔ Eliminate surprises later on in the project.

✔ Manage stakeholder expectations about what will be spent.

✔ Include a contingency for risks.

The difference between your actual estimate and the high end of the range gives you a pool of contingency money for expenses you have not predicted. In other words, it allows for Murphy to show up and still allows you to meet your budget. Just as it was important to have some contingency time in your schedule, it's just as important to have some contingency money in your budget. You can't predict the future precisely and your estimate needs to take that fact into account.

Once you have calculated the range, you'll need to compare the high end of the range to the spending limit that was given to you in the charter. If the high end of your spending range is below the spending limit, then your spending estimate is complete. However, if the high end of the range is above the spending limit, you need to

✔ Check your calculations to see if your assumptions and your calculations are correct.

✔ Check with the sponsor to see if there is any leeway in the spending limit. If cost is the number one priority for the project, then it's unlikely there is room for negotiation on the limit. If cost is the last priority, then you might get lucky.

✔ If the spending limit cannot be changed, you'll need to look for ways to reduce costs. This usually means one of three things: Convert outside effort into staff effort (if external costs are the concern), increase the risk of the project by eliminating countermeasures that cost money, or reduce the scope of the project. Ask your sponsor which option he or she is most interested in having you pursue or provide the sponsor with several options to pick from. For example, "We can reduce the scope of the final deliverable to X, or we can accept more risk by eliminating the following countermeasures, which will save us Y dollars, or we can add Z staff effort time to the project in order to save Y dollars in outside fees."

Before you document your results, do a content and process check to make sure you haven't forgotten anything.

Content and Process Check

- ❏ Did you ask the sponsor if you needed to estimate internal costs?
- ❏ Did you include project management time in your staff-effort estimate?
- ❏ Did you estimate all the external costs associated with your project?
- ❏ Did you estimate the accuracy of the spending estimate and calculate a range?
- ❏ Do you have consensus from the team on the estimate?
- ❏ Is the high end of your range under the spending limit? If not, has your sponsor given you the okay to go ahead or has the sponsor raised the spending limit?

THE PROJECT PLAN DOCUMENT

In order to document your spending estimate, you may want to complete a spending estimate form like the one shown in Figure 9.1. Enter the spending totals, the accuracy rating and range, and explain the reason for the accuracy rating. This will communicate to your stakeholders how you came up with your numbers and why the actual amount you spend may

153

SPENDING ESTIMATE FORM	
Project Name:	Project Sponsor:

Type of Expense	Cost
Internal Costs	
Indicate costs for internal charges. Staff effort costs	
would be included here. This section can be skipped	
if an organization is not capturing internal costs.	
SUBTOTAL:	
External Costs	
List any expenses that will require money being	
spent outside the organization. These expenses	
normally require a purchase order.	
SUBTOTAL:	
INTERNAL & EXTERNAL TOTAL:	
ACCURACY RATING*:	Rate the accuracy of the estimate.
RANGE:	Put a range on the total number, based on accuracy rating.
TOTAL COST SPENDING LIMIT:	If the sponsor provided a limit on spending, put that number here.

* Document reasons for each accuracy rating:

FIGURE 9.1 Spending estimate form.

be different. It will also serve as a reminder to you at the end of the project about what assumptions you used to create the estimate.

If you don't have to estimate internal costs, leave the top part of the form blank. This form will be one of the pieces of information that you include as you assemble the project plan document.

Chapter

10

Assembling the Project Plan

Congratulations. You've completed the planning activities and now it's time to assemble the plan. The project plan is the output of the planning phase. It captures the information you have compiled with the team and lays out how the project will be executed. If the charter represents the expectations and wishes for the project, the project plan represents the projected reality. Therefore, it's the plan that you will use to guide the project as you move forward into execution.

If you've followed our directions during the planning phase and involved the team and key stakeholders in the decision-making process, you shouldn't have too many surprises as you attempt to get the plan approved. If you constructed the plan in isolation, you'll have a much more difficult sell at this point in the project.

Before we discuss the sections of the plan document, let's review the CORE PM method to see how all the pieces fit together.

SCOPE PLAN

The scope plan defines what will be produced for the customer. You started with a description of the final deliverable, including its features and functions. Then you worked with the customer to define their acceptance criteria. These customer acceptance criteria (CAC) comprise the target for your project. The final deliverables must meet the CAC. The CAC are the customer's definition of what a successful final deliverable will be and the project team's way of knowing they are on the right track to be successful. The final deliverable must help to resolve the customer need or problem—the driving force for the project.

You also defined the boundaries of the scope—what's included and what's not—where overlaps exist, and when the project will end (see Figure 10.1). Finally you identified your list of stakeholders.

PROJECT ORGANIZATION

In order to produce the final deliverable, you had to organize the work of the project. You broke down the final deliverable into interim deliverables and someone on the team was assigned accountability for each one. Then you defined the subprojects and assigned each deliverable (interim and final) to a subproject.

Finally you needed to make sure you had the right people on the team. You assessed the skills you needed to create the deliverables and reviewed your list of stakeholders to make sure they had representation on the team or a team member liaison assigned to keep them involved in the project. You then made whatever adjustments were needed to get

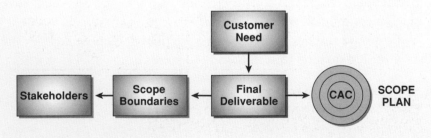

Figure 10.1 Scope plan.

156

the right team for the project (see Figure 10.2). You assigned someone from the team to manage each subproject.

RISK

During the risk assessment process, you and your team examined the final and interim deliverables and asked yourselves, "What could go wrong?" The risks for the project were identified and analyzed (see Figure 10.3). Then you created countermeasures to prevent these risks from occurring. The countermeasures were added to the schedule. The staff-effort time required to implement the countermeasures was added to the staff-effort estimate. Any costs associated with the countermeasures were included in the spending estimate.

RESOURCE PLANNING

The final question you addressed was, "How much time, effort, and money will it take to complete the project?" You developed a milestone schedule that will be used to communicate the highlights of

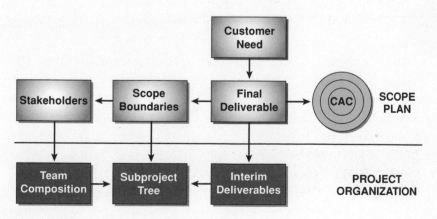

Figure 10.2 Project organization plan.

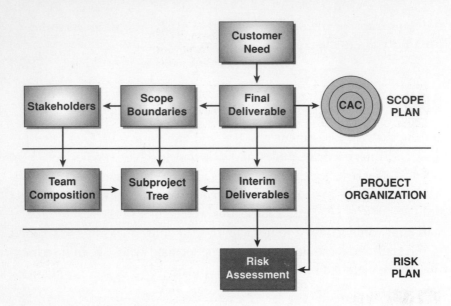

Figure 10.3 Risk plan.

your schedule to those outside the team. Then you created a deliverables schedule that shows the delivery date of each deliverable and the interdependencies between the deliverables. You included some contingency time at the end of the schedule to cover unexpected problems.

You estimated the staff-effort time to create each deliverable. Then you added the project management effort to the effort required to create the deliverables to get a total staff-effort estimate. The staff-effort time was converted to staff-effort cost, one of the internal costs for the project. Finally, you listed all the internal and external costs associated with the project and produced a spending estimate, with an accuracy rating and a range. (See Figure 10.4.)

That's it. All the pieces fit together in a nice logical flow. You'll need just one more document and you're ready to assemble the project plan. That document is the change-management plan.

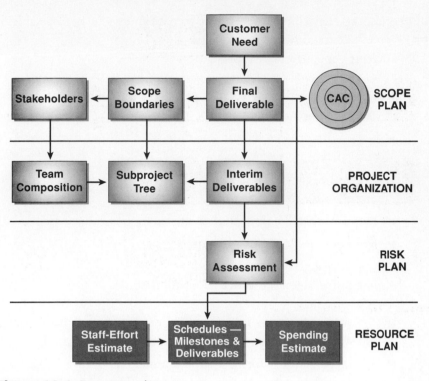

Figure 10.4 Resource plan.

CHANGE-MANAGEMENT PROCESS PLAN

You'll need a change-management process to handle any requests for changes to the project plan once it has been approved. Without a formal process for handling changes, you're likely to run into the problem of scope creep, which occurs when the customer and others continue to add things to the scope once the project plan is approved. "While you're producing this feature, can you also get the program to do _____?" This is an example of how scope creep gets started. Even without scope creep, projects often experience some need to change the scope or even the schedule or budget while the project is being executed. This is because not only can't we accurately predict the future,

159

but conditions may change during the project and we need to be able to make course corrections as we proceed.

A change-management process

- ✔ Forces evaluation of each request so that changes are not assumed to be automatic.
- ✔ Keeps the project scope, schedule, and budget under control and current.
- ✔ Helps the team to differentiate between necessary changes and unnecessary ones.
- ✔ Requires that the impact of each change be evaluated.
- ✔ Keeps the project plan current.

A change-management process should include

- ✔ A description of the change-management process. This shows the steps that will be taken when a change is requested.
- ✔ A change request form. This is completed by the person requesting the change to the project plan. This might be the customer or it could be the project team, if, for example, it is determined that a deadline date cannot be met or a feature of the final deliverable cannot be created.

In addition, the project leader will need a change log to track the status of each requested change.

THE CHANGE-MANAGEMENT PROCESS

There are two basic ways to convey the change-management process: through a flowchart and/or through a written description of the steps.

The steps in a generic change-management process are shown in Table 10.1.

A generic change-management process flowchart is shown in Figure 10.5.

These three steps are primarily managed using a change-request form, which has three parts: the request for a change that includes an explanation of why the change is needed (the justification section), an analysis of the impact of the change on the project (impact analysis section), and a section for approvals (approval section) (see Figure 10.6). The justification section is completed by the person requesting the change—this could be the customer, the sponsor, the project team, or another stakeholder. Or, if the request is sent to the team via e-mail or a phone call, the justification section is completed by the project leader

TABLE 10.1 Change Management	
Step	*Action*
1 —Request	Someone inside or outside the project team requests a change. The justification section of a change-request form is completed. The project team determines if the change makes sense. If the change requested does make sense, they proceed to step two. If the change requested does not make sense, then the issue with the change is recorded on the issues list and discussed with the sponsor and the person requesting the change.
2 —Impact	The team analyzes the change request and assesses the impact to the project. The impact analysis is reviewed with the originator, customer, and sponsor.
3 —Approval/ denial	The sponsor and customer either do or do not approve the change request. If the change request is not approved, the originator is notified of the denial. If the change request is approved, the originator and the team are notified and the project plan is amended.

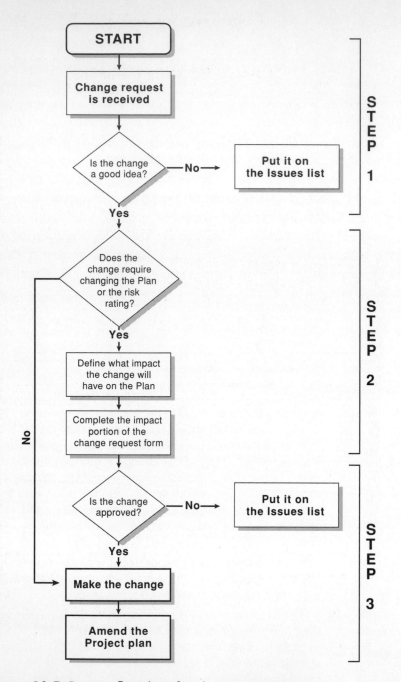

Figure 10.5 Process flowchart for change management.

CHANGE-REQUEST FORM

Project Name:	Project Sponsor:

The top part of the form is completed by the person requesting the change. The bottom half is completed by the project team. The change requested must be approved before it can be incorporated into the project plan.

STEP 1

JUSTIFICATION

		Urgency: How urgently is the change needed? High, medium, or low.	
Change Request #:	**Originator:**	**Change requested by:**	**Date requested:**
Assign a unique number to each change request.	Who completed the change-request form?	Who is requesting the change?	What is the date that the change-request form was completed?

Description of Change Request #:

What is the change that is being requested? Describe what needs to change.

Reason for Change:

What is the reason for the change? Why does the customer or the team need the change? What is the problem that the change request is supposed to address?

Proposed Approach to Resolve:

Is there a proposed approach to how to make the change? Explain that here.

STEP 2

IMPACT

PROJECT PLAN AREA	IMPACT OF PROPOSED CHANGE(S)
Impact on Scope	What changes will need to be made to the scope of the project? Are there new features or functions? Are the customer requirements changing? Are there new customer acceptance criteria?
Impact on Risk	What impact will there be on the risk? If there are new potential problems, indicate what the team would do to reduce the risks or their consequences.
Impact on Schedule	What change will need to be made to the schedule? What impact will there be on the deadline dates?
Impact on Spending	How much more money will be needed?
Other	Indicate any other impacts of the proposed change, i.e., changes needed to team composition, issues that could arise.

STEP 3

APPROVALS TO PROCEED:			
Originator/Date	Project Leader/Date	Sponsor/Date	Customer/Date

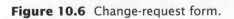

Figure 10.6 Change-request form.

163

and then signed by the person requesting the change. The project team completes the impact analysis section. The approval section is completed by those people who need to approve a change to the plan.

STEP ONE—THE REQUEST

When you or someone else wants to make a change to the project plan, the first thing that needs to be done is to complete the top section of the change-request form.

The justification section of the form addresses the following questions:

- ✔ What does the requestor want changed?
- ✔ Why does the requestor want it changed (what is the problem the requestor is trying to solve)?
- ✔ How does the requestor suggest you incorporate the change into the plan?
- ✔ How urgent is this request?

STEP TWO—THE IMPACT ANALYSIS

Next, assuming that the change is a good idea, the project team will need to analyze the change request and develop a proposed plan for handling the change. This involves having the team go back through the steps of planning to assess the impact of the change to the project plan. In this planning session, the team will have to evaluate the effect the change will have on scope, risk, and resources. For example, a change request to move the dinner/dance ahead a month would be analyzed in terms of the changes to scope (possibly changing the location or needing to find a different band); new risks that would be incurred; and changes in the risk assessment, changes to the budget, including the accuracy rating and range. The impact information is then captured on the impact section of the change form.

STEP THREE—APPROVALS

Finally, after the impact to the project is analyzed, the request must be approved if the project plan is to be amended. The people who need to approve the change vary from one company to the next, but typically the originator of the request, the project leader, sponsor, and customer must approve a change. If you require other approvals, make sure you include them on the form.

A change-request form, including instructions for completing it, should be included in the project plan.

THE CHANGE LOG

The project leader needs a method for tracking the status of each change request. For projects that receive very few change requests, this isn't much of an issue. However, some projects receive continual change requests and a formal system for tracking those change requests is required. This tracking is done via a change log. An example of a change log is shown in Figure 10.7.

Each change request is given a number. The originator of the request is recorded and the change that is being requested is described. The date the change request is received and the date a decision on the request is required are noted as well. You can also add a column to designate the urgency of the request.

Next, record the impact-analysis results. Describe the changes that will be made to the scope. For schedule impact, indicate the number of days, weeks, or months that will be added or deleted from the schedule. For spending impact, show the amount of increased or

PROJECT CHANGE LOG								
Project Name:				Project Sponsor:				
#	Originator	Description of Change	Date Received	Date Required	Scope Impact	Schedule Impact	Spending Impact	Approved? Yes/No
1								
2								
3								
4								

Figure 10.7 Change log.

decreased dollars in the budget. Finally, record the date the change was approved or disapproved.

Note: If you have the date the change request was received and the date it was approved, you can calculate the cycle time for each change request—the time it takes from when a change request is received until a decision is made on whether to proceed with the change.

This completes the change-management section of the project plan, and you're ready to move on to getting the entire project plan approved.

ASSEMBLE THE PROJECT PLAN

You should now have all the pieces you need to assemble the main body of the project plan. Review the list in Table 10.2 to see if you are missing anything.

You'll want to augment the plan with an executive summary.

EXECUTIVE SUMMARY

Limit the executive summary to one page. Some key things to include in the executive summary are shown in Table 10.3.

TABLE 10.2   The Project Plan Document

Section	Document or Form	Explanation
Initiation	Charter	Approved by the sponsor
Team	Team contract	The guidelines agreed to by the team
Scope	Scope description	A detailed description of what will be delivered to the customer
Scope	Customer acceptance criteria	The criteria the customer will use to determine if they are satisfied with the final deliverable
Scope	Scope boundaries	A description of what is inside and outside the scope of the project
Scope	Stakeholder form	A description of how each stakeholder will affect the project, the team status for each stakeholder, and the name of the team liaison, if one is required
Organization	Subproject tree	A diagram of all the subprojects, the person accountable, and interim deliverables for each subproject
Risk	Risk form	The identified risks, countermeasures, and the person accountable for each countermeasure
Resources	Milestone schedule	The high-level schedule for the customer, sponsor, and stakeholders
Resources	Deliverables schedule	The schedule showing interdependencies between the deliverables for the project team
Resources	Spending estimate	Internal and external costs, as required
Change management	Change-management process	The process by which changes to the project plan will be handled

TABLE 10.3 Executive Summary	
Step	*Action*
Project objectives	These should be taken from the charter, unless the objectives changed during the planning phase
Project customer	List the project customer
Key stakeholders	List the key stakeholders for the project (not including the customer and the sponsor)
Final deliverable	Describe the final deliverable
Customer acceptance criteria	List the customer acceptance criteria
Risks	List the main risks and the countermeasures you have chosen to reduce or eliminate these risks. Document the overall risk rating for the project. Document any key assumptions about the project—particularly assumptions related to technology or know-how.
Delivery date	Show the delivery date for the final deliverable.
Spending estimate	Provide the spending estimate, with the accuracy rating and range. Show the spending limit.
Project priorities	Show the priorities for the project: scope, schedule, and cost

After you've completed the executive summary, you're ready to gather approvals.

GETTING THE PROJECT PLAN APPROVED

You'll need to check with your sponsor to assemble a list of required signatures. Of course the sponsor is the first person who will need to approve the plan, and if you have an internal customer, the internal customer will need to approve it as well. It's usually a good idea to have the resource or functional managers sign off on the plan document as well.

168

Before you wrap up planning, do a quick content and process check.

Content and Process Check

❑ Have you written an executive summary for the project plan?

❑ Have you compiled all your project plan documents?

❑ Have you included a change-management process in your project plan? Does everyone (team, customer, sponsor) understand it?

❑ Has your plan been approved?

You're done! It's time to begin executing the project plan, and if you've done a good job of planning, you've set the foundation for a smooth-sailing project.

Chapter

Team-Based Tools

Y ou have now learned a whole set of team-based tools for managing projects such as the subproject tree, risk assessment, and the deliverables schedule. There are other, generic problem-solving tools that could be helpful to you during planning or executing your project.

These tools will help you to lead the team through the I.O.A.C.™ process of making a decision about just about anything:

✔ I = Identify ideas or concerns
✔ O = Organize the ideas
✔ A = Analyze the ideas
✔ C = Choose one or more options

There are a variety of tools available for each step in the I.O.A.C. process. We'll cover four tools that every project leader should have in his or her toolbox. These tools will address more than one of the steps in the I.O.A.C. process. For example, affinity diagramming, which was already covered briefly in Chapter 4 when we developed the team contract, incorporates both the identification (I) and organization (O) of ideas.

Decision making is a process of first diverging to explore the possibilities and then converging on a solution(s). To diverge is like the open end of a funnel, gathering as many ideas as possible. Convergence consists of narrowing down the choices. It's the narrow end of the funnel (see Figure 11.1). In between is organization and analysis, processes that help you select ideas that are both implementable and best fit the problem being experienced.

The I.O.A.C. process is best used in situations where

✔ There are a variety of ideas about how a problem should be approached and/or solved.

✔ Many people have concerns about a topic. (If only two people have concerns, you can use conflict resolution. However, if several people have concerns and their concerns are all different, then the I.O.A.C. process will help.)

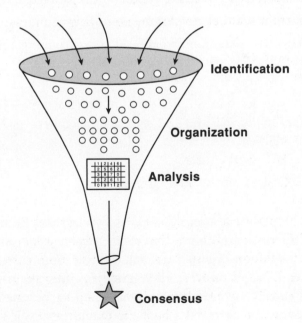

Figure 11.1 The I.O.A.C. funnel.

As you recall from our discussion in Chapter 3, team-based tools are ones that employ all three sensory learning styles: visual, auditory, and kinesthetic. They help to ensure that everyone is fully engaged in the decision-making process. They also lead the group to consensus so everyone can live with the decision that is selected.

Let's examine the first decision-making tool, the affinity diagram.

AFFINITY DIAGRAM (I, O)

The affinity diagram is a great tool for identifying and organizing ideas or issues. Use an affinity diagram when you need to

- ✔ Brainstorm with a large group.
- ✔ Organize a large number of brainstormed ideas into a format that can be used to take action on the problem.
- ✔ Encourage innovative connections between ideas.
- ✔ "Unstick" situations where old ways of doing things are not working, and new ideas seem hard to generate.

Before you begin an affinity-diagram exercise, tape a large piece of banner paper to the wall and give each team member a pad of self-stick notes and a marker.

Step 1

Begin the affinity-diagramming process by clearly defining the problem that you are attempting to solve. Then change the problem statement into a solution-oriented statement. For example, let's say you're working on a merger project and you're concerned about morale during the merger. The problem is potential low morale during the merger. A solution-oriented statement would be, "What are all the things we can do to maintain high morale during the merger?"

Step 2

Next, brainstorm all possible solutions. Brainstorming is an excellent way to get people thinking outside their usual patterns of thought and generating new ideas for solving a problem. Use these brainstorming guidelines to encourage the generation of ideas:

✔ All ideas are good ideas.

✔ Use self-stick notes to record ideas.

✔ Duplicates are okay.

✔ Go for quantity, not quality.

✔ Think outside the box—go crazy.

✔ No judgment.

✔ Don't stop and discuss.

✔ Keep the momentum going.

Use the Write it! Say it! Slap it!™ method of brainstorming discussed in Chapter 7. Each person writes his or her idea on a self-stick note, says it out loud, and then slaps it on the banner paper that has been taped to the wall. Generate as many ideas as possible. Go for wild and crazy solutions. This will help the group to think creatively. Each written idea should

✔ Include a noun and a verb.

✔ Be written with a marker.

✔ Be written in large enough print to be read from several feet away.

Continue brainstorming until you have exhausted the obvious ideas. Here are some hints for getting beyond the easy solutions:

✔ If the group has just a few ideas, they are probably high-level solutions. Use each of these high-level solutions as a topic for brainstorming. Convert it to a solution-oriented statement and brainstorm ideas that would address that high-level solution. Place the self-stick notes under the appropriate solution statement.

✔ Ask the group to generate some wild and crazy solutions to get outside the group's normal thinking. Ask questions such as, "If this solution were an onion, what would the solution look like?"

✔ Set stretch goals for the group. If they seem to have exhausted all their ideas, ask for 10 or 20 more. This will force them to think outside the box in order to reach the goal.

Step 3

The next step in affinity diagramming is to sort or organize the ideas. Have the team move to the banner paper to begin the sorting process. (It's best to do the sorting with groups of no more than six people.) The team then begins the organizing process in silence, which

✔ Reduces the influence of hierarchy in the group.
✔ Encourages people to focus on the ideas, not the people who wrote them.
✔ Forces each person to read each idea and make a connection between that idea and the other ideas. This objectifies the ideas, helping people to take ownership for all of the ideas instead of just the ones they generated.
✔ Eliminates the tendency to analyze or judge the ideas.
✔ Makes the process move faster.

The silence rule can be temporarily abandoned when there is a genuine lack of understanding of a particular idea. In that case, ask for a short explanation of the idea, but do not allow discussion of the idea.
Continue to sort the ideas until the group has finished moving the

self-stick notes around. They should now be in clusters on the banner paper. Here are some more tips on the organizing step:

✔ If a self-stick note is moved back and forth several times by two different team members, make a duplicate and place it in both locations.

✔ If a group of self-stick notes gets too big, more than 15 or so, subdivide it into subgroups.

✔ If there are outliers that don't seem to belong in any group, that's okay. Just make each one its own group.

The organizing step shouldn't take more than about 15 or 20 minutes unless you have a lot of self-stick notes (more than 100).

Step 4

Once the affinity notes are organized into groups, the group can begin to discuss what an appropriate header card for each group and each subgroup would be. The best way to create these header cards is to

✔ First, make a quick pass through the groups and create a draft header card with a one-word descriptor that captures the general idea of that grouping.

Tip: Use a different colored self-stick note for headers or use a larger size so they stand out from the ideas.

✔ Next, return to each draft header card and write a complete statement to describe the ideas in the grouping. The header should be about 5 to 10 words in length and it should be understandable without reading the ideas underneath it.

✔ Create header cards for any subgroups.

Review the header cards and the ideas underneath them. Discuss whether any additional subgroups are required. Decide if you need separate headers for the outliers or whether they belong in one of the existing groups (see Figure 11.2).

A summary of affinity steps is shown in Table 11.1.

That completes the affinity-diagramming exercise. You have generated ideas, organized them, and should have group consensus around the major categories.

The next stage in the I.O.A.C. process is to analyze the ideas and move the team to consensus. We'll discuss three basic tools to help you do that. The first one is the interrelationship digraph.

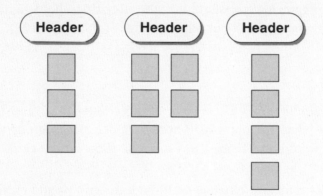

Figure 11.2 Affinity diagram.

TABLE 11.1 Affinity Diagramming	
Step	Action
1	Write a solution-oriented statement
2	Brainstorm ideas. Record on self-stick notes
3	Sort the ideas silently
4	Create header cards

INTERRELATIONSHIP DIGRAPH (A, C)

The interrelationship digraph (ID) allows you to diagram the cause and effect relationships between groups of the affinity or between up to ten potential solutions to a problem. Use the ID when you need to

- ✔ Separate symptoms from true causes.
- ✔ Identify the driving forces for change.
- ✔ Identify root causes of a problem or issue.

The interrelationship digraph is a great way to identify root causes for a problem. When evaluating potential solutions, the natural tendency is to focus on the obvious solutions or on solutions that will resolve the symptoms of the problem. The ID tool helps you to see beyond the symptoms to the root causes of either the problem or the solution.

Tape a piece of banner paper to the wall and ask the group (no more than six people in a group) to work at the wall. Provide them with markers and self-stick notes.

Step 1

Record the issue or problem statement on a self-stick note and place it at the top of the paper. This is slightly different than the solution-oriented statement you developed for the affinity diagram. In the ID, you're posing a question about the source of the problem or solution. For example, "What is the driving force that will help us avoid problems during the merger?"

Step 2

Assemble the causes you want to diagram. The causes can be generated by

✔ Using the categories of the affinity diagram.

✔ Brainstorming causes.

✔ Gathering data as to causes.

It's best to keep the total number of causes to 10 or less. If you have more than 10 causes, see if there is any way you can combine them to create a total of 10. Write each cause on a self-stick note and arrange in a circle on the banner paper (see Figure 11.3).

Step 3

Compare each pair of self-stick notes. For each pair ask, "Is one of these a cause of the other?" If one of the two is a cause, then the other is an effect of that cause, which creates a cause-and-effect relationship between the two. When this occurs draw an arrow from the cause to the effect. Do not draw two-headed arrows. If there is no clear cause-and-effect relationship between the two, don't draw any arrows.

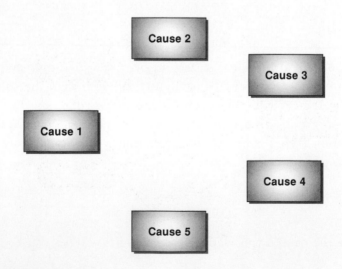

Figure 11.3 ID step two.

Continue analyzing each pair, working your way around the circle until every pair has been analyzed.

Step 4

Tally the number of outputs (arrows going out) and inputs (arrows coming in) for each self-stick note. For example, a tally of $^4/_2$ means there are four outputs and two inputs for that particular self-stick note (see Figure 11.4). The self-stick notes with the most outputs are root causes. Those with the most inputs are major effects or symptoms.

Step 5

Rearrange the self-stick notes with root causes on the left (self-stick notes with the most outputs) and major effects (self-stick notes with the most inputs) on the right. Place the rest of the self-stick notes in between. Redraw the arrows to represent the major relationships between

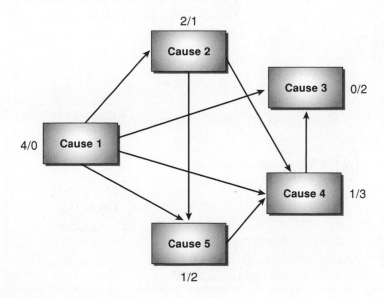

Figure 11.4 ID step four.

the issues (see Figure 11.5). You don't need to redraw every arrow that you drew in step 3. Instead, draw arrows representing the major connections between the causes and the effects.

It's usually best to first implement root causes and then intermediate causes. The major effects will probably be taken care of if you address the causes. A summary of interrelationship digraph steps is shown in Table 11.2.

If there is a question about which root cause you should work on, try one of the next two decision-making tools: the MT decision matrix or multivoting.

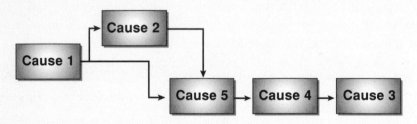

Figure 11.5 Completed ID.

TABLE 11.2 Interrelationship Digraph	
Step	*Action*
1	Write a problem statement
2	Assemble the causes
3	Compare each pair of causes for cause and effect relationships
4	Count the number of inputs and outputs for each cause
5	Redraw the ID with root causes on the left and major effects on the right

MT DECISION MATRIX (A, C)

When you need to decide among several viable solutions (or several root causes) and it's important to make the criteria for reaching the decision explicit, try the MartinTate (MT) decision-matrix tool.

Use the decision-matrix tool when

- ✔ You have a significant or complex decision to make.
- ✔ You want to analyze options based on a set of decision criteria.
- ✔ There is no consensus on what the best options are.
- ✔ One or more people seem biased about which option is best.
- ✔ You want to introduce more objectivity into the decision-making process.

Step 1

Create the decision matrix grid on banner paper. Label the two left-hand columns as shown in Figure 11.6, and label the top row as

	Weight	Decision Options		
Criteria				
DECISION SCORE				

Figure 11.6 MT decision matrix—step one.

shown. Write the goal to be achieved by the decision at the top of the banner paper.

Step 2

List the decision options across the top of the matrix. These decision options might have come from the headers in your affinity diagram or they could be root causes from the ID. Or, they might just be options that you brainstormed as a group. Discuss and write down clear descriptions of each, and ensure that everyone in the group understands them.

Suppose you are considering how to best implement project management training in your organization. You did an affinity diagram and came up with three options:

1. Classroom training with random enrollment—individuals sign up for prearranged training sessions.
2. Classroom training for project teams—intact project teams attend a prearranged workshop together.
3. Just-in-time training of project teams—training is divided into segments and the appropriate segment is taught when the team reaches that place in the project management process.

Step 3

Brainstorm a list of criteria that you'll use to make the decision. The criteria you choose should help you differentiate between the decision options. For example, a criterion that all students must learn the project management methodology isn't very useful if all three decision options satisfy the criterion.

The following are examples of decision criteria:

✔ Low cost
✔ Easy to implement

✔ Few barriers to implementation

✔ Short implementation timeline

Each option will be compared against each of the criteria chosen. It's best to have no more than six criteria. Use whatever criteria are appropriate to the decision you are trying to make. For each criterion write an operational definition of what the criterion means, so there is a shared understanding of the meaning of each criterion.

Step 4

If there are any yes/no criteria, such as "Option is feasible" or "Training will cost less than X dollars," run the decision options through those yes/no criteria and eliminate the no's. List the remaining criteria down the left-hand column of the decision grid (see Figure 11.7).

Criteria	Weight	Decision Options		
		Random enrollment in classroom	Project teams enroll in classroom	Project teams — JIT
Ease of scheduling trainer				
Minimize time away from work				
Apply to real projects				
DECISION SCORE				

Figure 11.7 MT decision matrix—step four.

Step 5

Establish a weight for each criterion. Use the 1 to 9 scale to give each criterion a weight:

Weights of 1 to 3 = Nice to have

Weights of 4 to 6 = Highly desirable

Weights 7 to 9   = Must have

It's best if each criterion has a different weight. For example, if you have two criteria that are highly desirable, give one a weight of 4 and the other a weight of 6 (see Figure 11.8). If the team has trouble reaching consensus on a criterion weight, ask each person to weight the criterion individually, and then pool and average the results. Check to make sure that the average weights make sense to the group. Make sure you have consensus before moving forward.

Criteria	Weight	Random enrollment in classroom	Project teams enroll in classroom	Project teams — JIT
		Decision Options		
Ease of scheduling trainer	1			
Minimize time away from work	3			
Apply to real projects	7			
DECISION SCORE				

Figure 11.8 MT decision matrix—step five.

Step 6

Cover up the criterion weights you just recorded with self-stick notes and then rate each decision option against each criterion. Use the following rating scale:

1 = the decision option does not satisfy the criterion

3 = the decision option satisfies the criterion moderately well

9 = the decision option satisfies the criterion extremely well

This 1, 3, 9 rating scale will help to differentiate the decision options that highly satisfy a criterion from those that only don't satisfy it or only moderately satisfy it.

Write the rating in the top left-hand corner of the cell (where the decision option and the criterion cross) (see Figure 11.9). The team should rate the options as a group. If consensus cannot be reached through discussion, ask each person to rate the decision options versus each criterion and then use the average. When you've finished the ratings, test for consensus.

Criteria	Weight	Random enrollment in classroom	Project teams enroll in classroom	Project teams — JIT
Decision Options				
Ease of scheduling trainer	1	3	3	1
Minimize time away from work	3	1	1	3
Apply to real projects	7	1	3	9
DECISION SCORE				

Figure 11.9 MT decision matrix—step six.

Step 7

Multiply the ratings (in the upper left corner of the cell) by the criteria weights (second column from the left), and record the total in the bottom right-hand corner of the cell (see Figure 11.10).

For each decision option, add the right corner numbers together and write the total at the bottom of the column. The column with the highest number is the solution that has performed best in light of the team's criteria. Discuss this as a team and decide if this is the best solution based on the goal statement at the top. If the solution doesn't make sense, review the criteria, the weights you gave each one, and the ratings. A summary of MT decision-matrix steps is shown in Table 11.3).

If it is not necessary to use an analytical approach to making the decision, you might want to opt for a faster, simpler decision-making tool, called multivoting.

		Decision Options		
Criteria	Weight	Random enrollment in classroom	Project teams enroll in classroom	Project teams — JIT
Ease of scheduling trainer	1	3 / 3	3 / 3	1 / 1
Minimize time away from work	3	1 / 3	1 / 3	3 / 9
Apply to real projects	7	1 / 7	3 / 21	9 / 63
DECISION SCORE		13	27	73

Figure 11.10 MT decision matrix—step seven.

TABLE 11.3 MT Decision Matrix	
Step	*Action*
1	Create decision matrix grid
2	List the solution options
3	Brainstorm a list of decision criteria
4	Filter options through "Yes/No" criteria
5	Establish a weight for each criterion
6	Compare each decision option against each criterion
7	Multiply the rankings with the criteria weights and generate a total for each decision option
	The option with the highest number is the winner.

MULTIVOTING (A, C)

Multivoting allows you to quickly narrow down a set of options by asking each person to select the decision options that he or she prefers. Anytime you ask someone to choose, they consciously or unconsciously use their own criteria and weigh the importance of each criterion against the decisions to be made. Usually this internal analysis process isn't very conscious to people and is totally invisible to the group, which is a distinct downside.

However, not every decision requires the level of analysis that is required in the decision matrix. Use multivoting when

✔ You want to get a quick feel for group consensus.
✔ The decision is not worth spending time on a more thorough analysis.

✔ You want to check if you already have consensus on a decision.

✔ The criteria for making the decision are well known and accepted by everyone on the team.

✔ You want to narrow down a long list of ideas to a selected few and then apply another analysis tool, such as the ID or MT decision matrix, to make the final decision.

Step 1

Provide each person on the team with stick-on dots. If you have 10 or more decision options, provide each person with 5 stick-on dots. If there are fewer than 10 options, divide the number of options in half and give each person that number of dots.

Step 2

Ask each person to think about the criteria he or she will use to make his or her decision. Then ask each person to vote for the decision options that he or she feels are the best. One dot, one vote. Do not place more than one dot on any one option.

Step 3

When the voting is complete, count the number of dots for each option. Rank the options from highest to lowest votes. Check to make sure this ranking makes sense to the group.

Before making a final decision, you can

✔ Pick the highest ranking option as the decision for the group.

✔ Weigh the strengths and weaknesses of the top two or three options, and then choose one.

✔ Use the top choices in another analysis tool, such as the interrelationship digraph or the MT decision matrix.

TABLE 11.4 Multivoting	
Step	Action
1	Provide each person with stick-on dots
2	Have each person vote for their top decision options
3	Count the votes

TOOLS FOR THE I.O.A.C. PROCESS

The four basic team-based tools that we've covered in this chapter—affinity diagramming, the interrelationship digraph, MT decision matrix, and multivoting—will provide you with the basic toolset you'll need to help the team make the best possible decisions during both the planning and the execution phases of the project. Speaking of execution, it's time to get on with producing those deliverables!

NOTES

More information on the Affinity Diagram, Interrelationship Digraph, and Multivoting can be found in the Memory Jogger II™, published by GOAL/QPC.

Executing the Plan

A fter the project plan is approved, it's time to create the final deliverables. In most projects, team members or subproject team members go off and work on producing their own deliverables. Most of the execution phase involves creating the deliverables, so hopefully, you've got a good project plan to work from because not only is execution the longest phase, but it also consumes most of the resources—time, effort, and money—for the project. If you followed the instructions in the prior chapters on project planning, you'll be in great shape as you move into the execution phase.

As the work is getting completed, there are four basic project management activities that you will need to perform:

✔ Monitor the environment.
✔ Manage change.
✔ Track progress.
✔ Communicate progress.

These four activities are primarily done during the project team meetings, which are periodic meetings with the team to make sure the project stays on track. The frequency of the meetings will depend on the length of the project and the amount of activity going on. Here are some guidelines for determining how frequently you should have team meetings:

✔ If your project is less than six months in length, then consider weekly or biweekly meetings.

✔ If your project is longer than six months in length but less than a year, you'll probably need biweekly meetings.

✔ If your project is longer than a year, consider biweekly or monthly meetings.

At each team meeting, you'll review the deliverables that were completed since last time and look ahead to deliverables scheduled for completion before the next team meeting. A general rule of thumb is that you shouldn't have more than six deliverables completed between one team meeting and the next. If there are more than six deliverables scheduled to be completed before the next team meeting, consider adding another meeting to your schedule.

There is no straightforward rule about how often to have team meetings. You're better off starting with more frequent meetings and then backing off if they aren't needed.

WHO SHOULD ATTEND?

The team meeting should include the project leader, the members of the main project team, and any ad hoc members who have been invited to the meeting. If you have a small project, the members of the main project team will be the people doing the work. If you have a large project, the project team members will consist of subproject team leaders. These subproject leaders should meet with their subproject teams, covering the same agenda items, before they attend the main project team meeting.

Before the team meeting, project team members should prepare a status update on their portion of the project. That means each team member should be prepared to report on the progress of his or her portion of the scope, risk, schedule, budget, and so forth. Before we discuss what should be in the status updates, let's first take a look at a typical agenda for either a project team or subproject team meeting.

TEAM-MEETING AGENDA

You'll be covering more or less the same topics each time you meet with the team. Here's a sample agenda for a team meeting during execution:

- ✔ Review the current status of the project—Team members report on the status of their portion of the project. Complete the status report form.

- ✔ Discuss potential problems—Monitor the environment for any new, potential problems that were not anticipated in the risk assessment. Decide what to do about problems that might occur. Complete the status report form.

- ✔ Review requests for changes to the plan—Review the justification and develop an impact analysis for pending change requests. Complete the status report form.

- ✔ Review and update the issues list—Discuss the resolution of pending issues. Add any new issues to the list. Complete the status report form.

- ✔ Clear the parking lot—Resolve parking-lot issues or move them to the issues list.

- ✔ Recognize accomplishments—Thank team members for the work that has been done. Recognize accomplishments.

- ✔ Evaluate the meeting—Do a quick check on how well the meeting was conducted so that it can be improved for the next time.

Let's examine how to work through each of these meeting agenda items. (They aren't presented in the same order as you'll cover them in your team meeting.)

MONITOR POTENTIAL PROBLEMS

Although you attempted to predict what would occur during the execution phase of the project, you're not psychic, and, therefore, you'll need to continually monitor the environment within and around the project to see if anything has changed since your risk exercise. Maybe there has been a change in the customer's organization. Or maybe a competitor announced a new product that is very similar to the one you are developing. Any new or different occurrence from what you expected should be evaluated.

Monitoring potential problems is not only done in the team meetings but also in review meetings with key stakeholders, such as with the customer and sponsor. Ask if anything significant has changed that could affect the project. Keep your antennae out at all times so you'll pick up information that will help you avoid problems with your project. If something in the environment does change, work with the project team to determine the type of impact it could have on the project.

✔ If there is an immediate impact, evaluate the nature and extent of the impact. Determine if you need to change the project plan. If a change is required, then use your change-management procedures.

✔ If the change could create a future impact, then you'll need to add it to your risk assessment. If the change in risk requires new countermeasures that would change the plan, implement your change-management procedures.

REVIEW STATUS

Reviewing the current status of the project allows you to track the progress of the project against the project plan, which simply means comparing where you are now versus where you planned to be, and then determining what you need to do if the project is veering off track.

The purpose of tracking progress is to ensure that you complete the project as promised: that the final deliverable meets the customer's acceptance criteria, that the project is on time and on budget. If you monitor the project regularly, you won't get very far off track without knowing it, and that gives you an early warning signal that allows you to take action to get back on track.

There are six areas you'll want to track:

✔ Risk
✔ Scope quality
✔ Schedule
✔ Staff effort
✔ Spending
✔ Changes to the plan

You'll note that these are all parts of the project plan. For each section track what is versus what was supposed to be at any point in time and then decide what to do about any deviations from the plan.

Note: Project organization is not tracked since it stays pretty constant unless there is a change in the scope of the project or a change within the company that requires a reassessment of the composition of the team.

Risk

As already discussed, you'll be monitoring the environment to detect any new risks or detect a change in your assumptions about the risks you identified earlier. When and if your original risk assumptions change or if you identify new risks, you'll need to add new countermeasures (which may require a change request), delete planned countermeasures (maybe the probability of a risk occurring has decreased and you no longer need the countermeasures), or add new risks to your assessment (which may also require a change request). Any changes in the risk assessment for the project should be noted on the status report (Figure 12.1).

RISK STATUS		
New Risks or Changes to Risk Assumptions	Action Plan	Change Request Required?

Figure 12.1 Risk section of status report.

Schedule

When you monitor the schedule you are asking, "Have you accomplished what you intended to accomplish by this point in time and do you expect to be on time in the future?" You'll monitor both milestones and deliverables, in the past and looking forward into the future. Looking back, have you met your milestone dates? How do the actual dates compare to the planned dates? Have you delivered the interim deliverables on time? How do the actual delivery dates compare to the planned delivery dates?

Looking forward, do you expect to meet your future milestone dates? If not, when do you expect to complete the milestone? What is the projected date of delivery for each interim deliverable scheduled for completion between now and the next team meeting?

Your schedule status is recorded on the status-report form (see Figure 12.2).

Note: Leave the last column blank (in the Deliverables Completed Since Last Update section of the status report) until you review scope quality.

If you see the schedule is starting to slip, work with the team to determine what might be causing the problem and brainstorm with the team members how to get the project back on track. Not every actual or projected slip in a delivery date will affect the project deadline; so focus your energy on potential changes that do jeopardize the deadline date—the ones on the critical path. Minor deviations from projected dates are expected. Major deviations that may cause you to miss your

SCHEDULE & SCOPE STATUS

Milestone	Planned Date	Actual Date	Projected Date

Deliverables completed since last update

Deliverable	Person Accountable	Actual Date	Met Quality Criteria?

Deliverables scheduled for completion

Deliverable	Person Accountable	Scheduled Completion Date	Projected Completion Date

Figure 12.2 Schedule section of status report.

deadlines need your attention. Detect these potential deviations early so you can prevent the schedule from slipping.

Scope Quality

The scope quality plan is the plan for how the team intends to meet the customer's acceptance criteria for the final deliverable. Effective project management does not include waiting until you deliver the final deliverable to the customer and then discovering that you have a quality problem. By the time that happens you have already disappointed the customer and you'll have to do rework in order to correct the problem. Rework is not only expensive, it adds additional time to the project.

Therefore, the best approach to assure that the final deliverable is acceptable is to assure each interim deliverable is acceptable to its customer in the chain. This is done by creating a scope plan and then monitoring the quality of the deliverables as they are produced throughout the project.

Each time an interim deliverable is completed and handed off to the internal customer for the deliverable, ask him or her if they are satisfied with the quality of the deliverable.

If the internal customer is satisfied with the interim deliverable, then indicate acceptance with a check mark on the status report form. If the interim deliverable does not meet the criteria, then the person supplying the deliverable will need to make whatever changes are required to get the deliverable up to the quality standards required. Indicate on the status report form your plan of action for correcting the quality of the deliverable.

Tip: It's a good idea to agree on the quality or acceptance criteria for interim deliverables before you begin producing them. This can be done during planning. It's only necessary to define quality or acceptance criteria for deliverables you haven't produced before or for ones that, in the past, did not satisfy the internal customer.

Staffing and Spending

If you included staff effort and spending in your project plan, you'll need to monitor the actual staff effort and cost versus the planned amounts. Even if you didn't include them in the plan, it's not a bad idea to monitor them anyway, so that you can begin to amass an historical record of what it takes to complete a certain type of project. Staffing effort actuals, the amount of time that has been spent on the project, are recorded on the status report form. Spending actuals versus the spending plan are also recorded. The actuals tell you what you have spent to date, but don't tell you if you're on track to meet the planned budget unless you periodically reproject how much you still have to spend to complete the project. Let's suppose you have a spending budget of $400 and the project is four months long. After the first month, you've spent

197

$125. Are you on budget? Over? Under? You may be on budget if more of your expenses were to be incurred in the beginning of the project. On the other hand, if most of the expenses will be incurred late in the project, you're probably running over budget. The way to find out if you're on budget or not, is to ask the team for a forecast of what they need to spend to finish the project. Add this forecast to what has already been spent for a new spending estimate. For example, let's say that your team projects they will spend another $275 (medium accuracy) to complete the project. You place a range on the projected spending number of $250 and $300. You add the $300 projection to the $125 already spent, giving you a projected total that is $25 over budget. Not good. You have several options if you find you are projected to be over budget:

- ✔ After you've discussed the situation with your sponsor, complete a change request for more funds.
- ✔ If you're in the beginning of the project, do nothing and continue to monitor spending to see if the actual spending is lower than the projections.
- ✔ Investigate where you can cut expenses or how you might reduce scope.

If you find you will run over budget, talk to your sponsor as soon as possible. The sponsor probably doesn't like surprises and he or she might have some ideas on how to get spending back on track.

Record your staff effort and spending actuals on your status report (see Figure 12.3).

REVIEW REQUESTS FOR CHANGES

If you determine that you will not be able to meet the promises you made in the project plan or if a key stakeholder wants you to change the plan—that is, add features or functions to the final deliverable, add

STAFF EFFORT & SPENDING STATUS			
	Total Plan Amount	*Actual to Date*	*Projected Total*
Staffing			
Spending			

Figure 12.3 Staff effort and spending sections of the status report.

a new deliverable, shorten the schedule, reduce the budget—then you'll need to employ your change-management process.

First, a change-request form must be completed. The person requesting the change should complete the top portion of the change-request form (see Chapter 10). When you receive the change request, give it a number and record it on your change log. If you recall, this is merely a record of each change request that is received and the status of the change request. Let's suppose you receive a change request for your dinner/dance project to add 50 more guests to the attendee list. The justi-fication is that one of the vice presidents has identified additional people who worked on the project and he or she feels they should be included in the celebration event.

Next, ask the team to consider if the change being requested is a good idea or not. If the change does not make good common sense, then go back and discuss the change request with the sponsor. If the sponsor agrees the change is not a good idea, then you'll need to dis-cuss the change request with the person who requested it. Maybe he or she has more information on why the change is important than was supplied with the request form. The next step, evaluating the impact to the project of a requested change, will take project resources—at least time and effort—and you don't want to expend those resources for re-quests that don't make sense. So, before you do the impact analysis for a change, make sure it makes sense.

Next, evaluate the impact of the change on the approved project plan. We would evaluate the impact of increasing the dinner/dance at-tendee list by 50 people. We would evaluate the impact to

✔ Scope (it may require we move to a larger venue, for example).

✔ Risk (more people may increase certain risks or create new ones).

✔ The resource plan—does it affect the schedule, staff effort, spending?

Let's take another example. Suppose the sponsor wants to reduce the budget by $2,500. In our impact analysis, we would evaluate ways of reducing costs, such as moving the reception inside to save on the cost of a tent or we might be able to convert outside labor to internal labor (ask for volunteers). We could reduce costs by eliminating countermeasures or we might offer several options for how we could reduce the scope to accommodate the cost reduction, such as having a buffet dinner instead of a sit down affair.

In order to develop the impact analysis, you'll need to conduct a miniplanning session with the team, working through each of the planning areas again, asking the question, "How will the requested change impact the current plan?" Once you've completed the impact section of the change-request form, the sponsor and customer must approve the change.

If the change is approved, then the project plan is amended and the amended plan becomes the new official plan. Moving forward, all progress on the project should be tracked against the new amended plan.

If the change is denied, then you'll need to return the change-request form to the person who requested the change and explain to him the reasons for the denial. It's usually best to do this in person or at least over the phone, so that you have a chance to answer any questions the person might have. If the person who requested the change is at a higher level in the organization than you and you feel you need support in delivering the bad news, ask your sponsor to help. That's what the sponsor is there for.

Complete the change-request section of the status report by indicating the change that was requested, the date the change was received, whether the change was approved, and if it was approved, the changes made to the project plan (see Figure 12.4).

REVIEW AND UPDATE THE ISSUES LIST

Review the issues list with the members of the team. Discuss the resolution of issues that were scheduled to be completed by the team meeting. Record information on how the issue was resolved and the date. Discuss any issues that have not been resolved and develop a strategy for getting the issue resolved. If you need to escalate the issue, consider putting it on your status report (see Figure 12.5). Next, review issues that will need resolution before the next team meeting.

CHANGES TO PLAN			
Description of Change	Date	Change Approved?	Revision to Plan

Figure 12.4 Change-request section of status report.

ISSUES SECTION				
Issue	Action Taken	Action Required	Person Accountable	Required Date

Figure 12.5 Issues section of status report.

201

COMPLETE THE STATUS REPORT

You have been completing the status report as you reviewed project progress with the team. By this point, you already have a status report that's almost complete. The last section is a dashboard or summary section showing the overall status of the project (see Figure 12.6). Assess the overall status of scope quality, schedule, staff effort, and spending.

After the meeting, issue the status report to team members, the sponsor, the customer, and other stakeholders. It will also serve as minutes of the project team meeting. The status report is one of the key tools you have for keeping stakeholders apprised of the progress on your project.

CLEAR THE PARKING LOT

At the end of the meeting, go back to the parking lot and see if there are any items on it that have not been resolved. If there are remaining items, you can do any of the following:

✔ Discuss and resolve the issue or idea before closing the meeting.

✔ Put the issue on the issues list, assigning accountability to get the issue resolved.

DASHBOARD							
Overall scope quality:	—	Exceeds	—	On	—	Below	—	In jeopardy
Overall project schedule:	—	Ahead	—	On	—	Behind	—	In jeopardy
Overall staffing status:	—	Below	—	On	—	Over	—	In jeopardy
Overall spending status:	—	Below	—	On	—	Over	—	In jeopardy

Figure 12.6 Dashboard section of status report.

202

✔ Discard the issue if it's already been discussed or if the person who raised it is no longer concerned about it. It's common to have someone raise an issue early in a meeting and then have the issue discussed later, or to have an issue lose its significance because of other discussions. Always check with the person who raised the issue before discarding it.

✔ Put the issue on the agenda for the next project team meeting.

RECOGNIZE ACCOMPLISHMENTS

It never hurts to say thank-you to the members of the team for the work they've put in on the project. Most people are juggling several projects at a time. A simple thank-you will go a long way to making people feel appreciated and in helping you move the team forward to that high-performing stage of team development we talked about earlier.

In addition, as you hit major milestones, do something special to recognize the accomplishment. At the very least, recognize the work of the team. You might also consider bringing pastries or fruit to the meeting as a thank-you. Stopping briefly to recognize accomplishments will help to maintain momentum as you move through the project.

EVALUATE THE MEETING

Before you adjourn the meeting, do a quick check on what went well and what you could do to improve the meeting for next time. The simplest way to do this is to give each person self-stick notes and ask them to write down what they liked about the meeting and things they think could be improved for next time. Place two pieces of flip-chart paper next to the door. Label one *plus* for things that went well, and the other *delta* for things they'd like to change. As they leave the meeting, ask them to slap their self-stick notes on the appropriate piece of paper. This will provide quick feedback on how to improve your project team meeting.

REVIEW MEETINGS WITH THE CUSTOMER AND SPONSOR

In addition to conducting team meetings, you'll want to sit down periodically with the customer and sponsor and review the project with them. You don't need to have these review meetings as frequently as you have project team meetings; usually once a month will do. The sponsor/customer review meeting will give you a chance to address specific questions they might have and to get their inputs on any changes that might affect the project. You should also solicit their feedback on ways you might improve what you are doing.

Here are some tips for maintaining good relationships with your customers/sponsors:

✔ Keep them informed on the progress of the project and any anticipated project changes. This will help them feel confident in your ability to manage the project and they'll be less likely to try and micromanage the project for you.

✔ Let them know of problems as soon as possible. Don't let them hear it from someone else.

✔ Ask them for their input.

✔ Include the customer on the team, where appropriate.

✔ Hold them accountable for their commitments. When necessary, put their activities/commitments on the schedule so they are visible and the interdependencies are clear.

✔ Be honest with them.

✔ Give them enough objective information so they can make informed choices. Don't ask, "What do you want us to do?" Instead say, "If we do this, the cost will be x, the advantages/benefits will be y, and it will take z days or weeks. In other words, provide them with the consequences of their choices.

✔ Be clear when you are asking for help. Quantify your request without ambiguity so there is no misunderstanding. Getting the wrong help is like wasting a trump card.

✔ Offer alternatives/options, but don't make the decision for them.

At the end of each customer or sponsor review meeting, ask if their needs for this encounter were met or if they have any concerns. Their concerns may expose something that has not yet become visible to the team, giving you a chance to fix the problem while it's still small. Or, if the concern is the result of a misunderstanding, this is a chance to clarify the situation.

Finally, don't forget to thank them for their support.

DELIVERING THE FINAL DELIVERABLE

Continue to monitor progress with the team and review progress with the sponsor and customer until you've completed the final deliverable and delivered it to the customer. At this point, the execution phase of the project is over and it's time to move on to close out.

CONTENT AND PROCESS CHECK

Here's a list of content and process checkpoints:

❏ Are you monitoring the environment (competition, customer, technology, and so forth) for changes that could affect your project?

❏ Do you ask the sponsor and customer if there are changes in the environment that they are aware of?

❑ Do you regularly review potential problems at project team meetings?

❑ Are you using the change-management process that you included in the project plan?

❑ Are change requests logged into the change log?

❑ Is the team involved in assessing the impact on the project plan for each change that is requested?

❑ Do team members come to the team meeting prepared to report on project status?

❑ Are team members actively involved in making sure the project stays on track?

❑ Do team members still feel ownership of the project?

❑ Do you issue regular status reports?

❑ Are you having regular review meetings with the customer and sponsor?

❑ Are you asking the sponsor and customer for their feedback on their perceptions of the project's performance?

Chapter

Closing Out
the Project

After the customer accepts the final deliverable, you may think you're done. But not quite. You still have the last phase of the project management process to work through—close out. The purpose of close out is to wrap up the project and make sure you and the team learn from what transpired. If you did a good job of planning and execution, the close-out phase should be fairly simple and fun. In fact, every phase will be fairly simple and fun if the previous phase was done well.

Some project leaders avoid close out because there are unresolved problems with the project: There are unhappy customers or team members, overrun budgets, and late schedule dates. Close out is also difficult when team members have other project or job commitments that they feel are more important than wrapping up your project. But close out is important, even in these less than optimal situations. It is during close out that you compare how you did to what you said you were going to do, and you learn from that experience. It is also during close out that you get a true evaluation of the project by the customer, sponsor, other stakeholders, and team members. These evaluations are key to helping you learn from the project and develop recommendations that will help others in the organization avoid making the same mistakes in the future.

The close-out phase can be broken down into five types of activities: having the project evaluated, writing the final status report, developing lessons learned, issuing the close-out report, and reviewing the report with the sponsor.

CUSTOMER EVALUATION

After the customer has accepted the final deliverable, it's time to have the customer evaluate the project. This is best done through a survey form. What you'll want to include on the survey are statements that the customer can rate on a 1 to 6 or 1 to 10 scale of strongly disagree to strongly agree. (It's best to use an even-numbered scale so that the customer is forced to pick a number that is not in the middle. This will give you a better idea if he or she is positive or negative, rather than neutral.) Sample statements that explore the customer's opinion on the results of the project include:

- ✔ The final deliverables met my acceptance criteria.
- ✔ The final deliverables met my expectations.
- ✔ The delivery date met my needs.
- ✔ The cost met my needs.
- ✔ Overall, I was satisfied with the results of the project.

You will also want to include statements that explore the project management process, such as:

- ✔ The project plan was complete and effective.
- ✔ The scope of the project was well defined.
- ✔ The change-management process was effective.

✔ My level of involvement in the project fit my needs.

✔ Status reports were clear and complete.

✔ I was kept informed on the progress of the project.

✔ Overall, I was satisfied with the project management process.

Also add statements specific to your project to the list. For example, if you did a software implementation project, you might ask if the software training program was acceptable and what, if anything, could have been improved.

CUSTOMER INTERVIEW

After the customer completes the survey, it's time to sit down for a one-on-one interview. You may want to invite the sponsor to this meeting as well. During this meeting, there are two questions you'll need to explore: what went well (plus) and what could we do better next time (delta)? You can record their answers on a plus/delta form (see Figure 13.1).

As you can see, the topics on the form mirror the statements on the survey. The interview is your opportunity to probe for more detailed information from the customer relative to the survey. For example, if the customer rated the statement, "The scope of the project was well defined," as a three out of six, ask the customer what they liked about the scope definition and what they would suggest you do differently next time. Record the responses on the form.

It's important not to get defensive or to try and justify what did or did not happen during the project. Your job during this interview is to simply ask questions and record the customer's answers, not to defend your actions. Think of yourself as an impartial journalist who is just trying to gather information. If you want a chance to explain what happened, ask for a follow-up meeting.

209

PLUS/DELTA FORM		
Project Name:	Project Sponsor:	
PROJECT RESULTS	**Went Well (+)**	**Ideas for Improvement (Δ)**
Scope/deliverables		
Team composition		
Schedule		
Staffing		
Spending		
Risks		
PROJECT MANAGEMENT PROCESS		
Project initiation		
Project planning		
Monitoring		
Change control		
Communications		
Other		

Figure 13.1 Plus/delta form.

FINAL STATUS REPORT

Once you have the customer's evaluation of the project, you're ready to complete your final status report (see Figure 13.2). This is done in the same way as the interim status reports except:

✔ Add a scope section to describe how well the final deliverable met each of the customer's acceptance criteria.

FINAL STATUS REPORT

Project Name:	Project Sponsor:	Date:

Scope Status:		
Final Deliverable	**Acceptance Criteria**	**Results**

Schedule Status:		
Final Deliverable and Key Milestones	**Final Plan**	**Actual Completion**

Staffing & Spending Status:		
	Final Plan	**Actual Amount**
STAFFING		
SPENDING		

Changes to Plan: (Total Changes)			
	Original	**Change**	**Final Plan Amount**
SCOPE			
DEADLINES			
STAFFING EFFORT			
SPENDING			

Explain all variances:

Figure 13.2 Final status report.

211

✔ In the schedule section, list all of the major milestones with planned versus actual dates. If the final deliverable was not one of the milestones, add it to the list.

✔ In the staffing and spending section, summarize the actuals for staff effort and spending versus the final approved plan amount.

✔ In the changes to plan section, summarize the changes made to the original plan. The final plan section should match the final plan columns in scope (changes to acceptance criteria), schedule, staffing, and spending.

✔ In the bottom section, explain any variances of the final actuals from the final plan amount. A variance is a deviation or a change from what was planned. A variance can be positive— you completed the project ahead of schedule—or negative. It's just as important to explain positive variances as negative ones, so that you and others will understand the reasons for both your successes and your failures.

SPONSOR EVALUATION

Ask the sponsor to evaluate the project using the same method you used for the customer. First send him or her a survey form and then conduct an interview. Provide the sponsor with the final status report before you ask for their project evaluation.

Use essentially the same statements for your sponsor survey that you used for the customer (so you can compare results). In the project results section, you'll need to reword the statements slightly. For example, instead of saying the final deliverable met my expectations, you would write, "The final deliverable met the expectations of the customer." You can also add statements such as, "The final deliverable met the needs of the organization."

You'll also want to explore the project management process in more depth. Here are some additional statements that might be useful:

✔ The project planning process was thorough.

✔ The project planning process was efficient.

✔ The involvement of stakeholders in the project process was effective.

✔ The resources of the project were used efficiently.

✔ The changes made to the scope of the project could not have been anticipated during the planning process.

✔ The project leader did an excellent job.

✔ The issues that were escalated to the sponsor level were appropriate for sponsor intervention.

Add any additional statements that will provide you helpful information. After you get the survey back, conduct a sponsor interview in the same manner as the customer interview. Use another plus/delta form and record the responses from the sponsor.

OTHER STAKEHOLDER EVALUATIONS

It's also helpful to get feedback from the other stakeholders, such as the resource managers. Rather than conducting interviews with each one, combine the plus/delta form with a survey form and have them complete and return it.

To create a combined form, simply add two columns next to each survey statement, label one Went Well and the other, Ideas for Improvement. A sample form is shown in Figure 13.3.

You'll be primarily surveying them on the project management process. Use the same set of core questions that you used for the customer and sponsor. You can add some statements specific to them as well:

✔ I was adequately informed about what resources would be required for the project.

STAKEHOLDER EVALUATION FORM			
Project Name:	Project Sponsor:		
Survey Statement	Rating	Went Well (+)	Ideas for Improvement (Δ)
1. The project plan was complete and effective.	1 2 3 4 5 6		
2. The scope of the project was well defined.	1 2 3 4 5 6		
3. The change-management process was effective.	1 2 3 4 5 6		
4. My level of involvement in the project fit my needs.	1 2 3 4 5 6		
5. Status reports were clear and complete.	1 2 3 4 5 6		
6. I was kept informed on the progress of the project.	1 2 3 4 5 6		
7. The project planning process was thorough.	1 2 3 4 5 6		
8. The project planning process was efficient.	1 2 3 4 5 6		
9. The involvement of stakeholders in the project process was effective.	1 2 3 4 5 6		

Figure 13.3 Stakeholder evaluation form.

✔ I was kept informed on the progress of the project.

✔ I was satisfied with the level of input I had on the project.

✔ I was kept informed on project progress by my team representative.

If you have questions about a specific response, call and discuss it with the person involved. When you get the surveys back, collate the results into a single survey form that you can share with the team.

TEAM MEMBER EVALUATIONS

Ask your team members to evaluate the project. The survey you provide to them should address the following:

✔ The way in which the project was led. (These questions provide the leader with feedback about how well he or she performed.)

✔ The project management process, including the effectiveness of planning, monitoring, and change control.

✔ The team process—how well the team worked together, how productive the team meetings were.

✔ Organizational support of the project.

Use a survey format like the stakeholder survey so that team members have a chance to write down what they liked and what could be improved.

LESSONS LEARNED

Once you've obtained all the feedback, it's time to hold a lessons-learned meeting with the team. Bring the lessons-learned list that you compiled throughout the project, the final status report, the evaluations, and the plus/delta forms. As you review the final status report and feedback forms, record any new lessons learned on a piece of flip-chart paper so everyone can follow the discussion.

Note: Don't forget that this is a learning meeting; so don't let it degenerate into a session of placing blame for problems that have occurred. And, remember to look at your successes, as well as your failures, because there may be lessons you need to learn from them as well. We tend to focus on our mistakes and how to correct them, but it's equally important to analyze our successes to learn how to repeat them.

RECOMMENDATIONS FOR IMPROVEMENT

After you've captured the lessons learned, discuss how to turn them into recommendations for improving the overall project management system in the organization. The list of overall recommendations for improvement will be shorter than your lessons-learned list, because not all the lessons will apply across the board.

Include the recommendations for improving the overall project management system in your close-out report.

THE CLOSE-OUT REPORT

The close-out report is the final report for the project. It includes an executive summary, the final status report, the lessons-learned list, and any recommendations for improvement. After you've drafted the close-out report, schedule a meeting with the sponsor to review the report before it's issued. After you get the sponsor's okay, issue the report and archive all project documents. Just one last thing before you're done: Don't forget to celebrate.

CELEBRATING

Take a minute, or longer, to pat yourselves on the back for the good work you've done. There are lots of ways to celebrate—a luncheon, a pizza party, coffee and donuts. Whichever way you choose, have a closing ritual for the project. Thank the group and each person individually for their contributions. If the project was a success, you may want to do this in public. If the project wasn't a success, you should thank people nonetheless. They worked hard on the project and that hard work should be recognized.

If the project was successful and if you made it through to the performing stage of team development, you have all the more reason for a closing ritual, because now you've entered the mourning stage. People

216

are sad to leave the team. They've had a rewarding and enjoyable experience. These don't come along too often so there is sadness in letting go. Acknowledge the good times you've had together and say good-bye. This will help put closure on the project.

CONTENT AND PROCESS CHECK

The following checklist will help you focus on close out.

❏ Have you gotten honest feedback from your customer, sponsor, team members, and stakeholders about the deliverables produced and the project process?

❏ Has the final status report been completed?

❏ Has each member on the team evaluated the project?

❏ Have you discussed and assembled a list of lessons learned?

❏ Has the team reached consensus on the recommendations for improvement?

❏ Has the project leader discussed the recommendations with the sponsor before issuing the close-out report?

❏ Has the project leader thanked each member of the team?

❏ Has the team celebrated its successes?

## Chapter 14

Summing Up

W e've covered a lot of ground so far and if you've followed the steps in the CORE PM method, you should have reached the Emerald City. Now it's time to look back and review what you've learned. There are seven keys to creating a successful project.

THE SEVEN KEYS TO SUCCESS

The seven keys to creating a successful project focus on things that individual project teams can and should do to make their projects more successful. The seven keys to success are:

1. Use an effective method.
2. Invest in planning.
3. Involve the customer.
4. Make it manageable.
5. Develop the team.

6. Communicate effectively.

7. Learn from your mistakes.

Let's examine each of these individually.

KEY 1—USE AN EFFECTIVE METHOD

An effective method, such as the CORE PM method discussed in this book, provides you with the steps and tools you need to complete a project successfully. There is no real sense in inventing your own method, unless you're an expert in project management with tons of experience. You're better off using a method that's proven and focus instead on leading the team through its steps.

The most important element of the first key is the word *use*. No method is effective if it isn't used. The application of the method is what produces results. Reading about a method but not using it doesn't produce anything tangible. Try the tools and techniques you've just read about. Ask the rest of your team to read up on the method and then try it together. You don't have to use the entire method to start. Start by writing a charter or doing a risk assessment. Try creating a schedule with the team or completing a team contract. Whatever parts of the method you actually use will help to improve your projects.

KEY 2—INVEST IN PLANNING

Most project teams dive into execution without having a charter or developing a project plan. They think that getting started on creating the deliverables will shorten the time it takes to do the project. However, investing in planning will

✔ Help to ensure that the final deliverable will satisfy the customer.

219

✔ Help to avoid problems and minimize rework.

✔ Make sure you're headed in the right direction before you begin work.

✔ Make sure you've got commitment from management on your plan of action.

✔ Shorten the total time it takes to do a project.

There are three ways to invest in planning.

1. Investigate the customer need. Make sure you're solving the right problem for the customer and that the best possible solution for the problem is the one you're implementing. Continually check that your final deliverable will help the customer to solve the problem they are experiencing.

2. Never start a project without a charter. This document outlines the expectations of management—the direction for the project and any resource limitations that exist. Starting a project without a charter is like heading off on vacation without a destination in mind. That's great if you aren't expected at a certain time in a certain place, but not so great if you are. Management is expecting you to arrive at a destination. Find out what it is.

3. Create the project plan with the team. Make sure you've thoroughly defined the scope, the stakeholders, your risk plan, your schedule, and a budget. Get the plan approved by the sponsor, customer, resource managers, and any other key stakeholders. The project plan is your map for getting to your destination. It defines exactly where you're going, how many pit stops you intend to make, what your meal plan is—everything that you need to arrive safely at your destination.

KEY 3—INVOLVE THE CUSTOMER

Projects exist to satisfy a customer. Project teams often have difficulty identifying the customer, understanding clearly what the customer needs and wants, and then translating that set of wants into customer requirements that the customer can understand and agree to. The best way to ensure that the deliverable from the project meets the customer needs and wants is to involve the customer in the project process, particularly in the early stages when the scope of the project is being defined. This helps to avoid dissatisfied customers, scope creep, or continual changes to scope, and it also creates customer buy-in and ownership for the project and its results.

After you've gathered the customer's requirements and the customer has agreed to them, keep the customer involved in the project. Where appropriate, have a customer representative on the project team. In that way you'll get continual input from the customer. The team representative can also act as a team ambassador back to the customer.

During the execution phase, the project leader should meet regularly with the customer, reporting on progress and gathering feedback and information that might be important to the project. When problems arise, let the customer know you have an action plan to resolve the problem. If it's a problem that will impact the customer, first get customer input on how to resolve the problem. Offer several options to choose from. Then report back on how the implementation is progressing.

After the customer accepts the final deliverable, ask him or her to evaluate not only the results of the project but the process used to create the results.

Customers can be your best allies on projects. Use them wisely.

KEY 4—MAKE IT MANAGEABLE

It's easy to get overwhelmed. You have a goal to reach that seems unreachable. You have limited resources. You've got a group of people

221

who don't know what to do. Don't panic. Define the goal—the final deliverable—clearly. Break the goal down into pieces, interim deliverables, and then organize those into subprojects. Assign someone to oversee each subproject.

Making a project manageable means making it workable, and when a project is workable, it can get done.

In the CORE PM method we focus on deliverables (which are the results or outputs), instead of activities (which are the tasks in the process). Most other methods focus on activities. There are a number of benefits of working with deliverables:

- ✔ You can define clear accountability for a deliverable: who will get it done, by when, for how much money, by what quality standards.
- ✔ It's easy to monitor deliverables. They either got produced on time, within budget, and met the customer's acceptance criteria or they didn't.
- ✔ You don't get lost in the details. Larger projects can have so many activities that identifying interdependencies between activities is difficult. When the main project team focuses on deliverables and leaves the details to the subprojects, the interdependencies are clearer and can be managed more easily.

KEY 5—DEVELOP THE TEAM

One of the key roles of the project leader is to develop the team. Let's look at a couple of important elements of team development.

Involve the Team in Planning the Project

Building an effective team starts at kick-off. Assess what skills and stakeholder representation you'll need on the team and then use the team to help you develop the project plan. When you get to execution, have the team participate in keeping the project on track. Ownership by the team during execution will produce more commitment to solving problems that arise. They will retain ownership of the project and any problems will belong to the whole team, not just to the project leader.

Use Team-Based Visual Tools and Techniques

Team-based tools will help you engage the whole team in the project process. If you're used to conducting meetings where everyone sits around a table and talks, using team-based tools that engage all three sensory learning styles might feel uncomfortable at first. But once you start, you won't want to go back to the strictly auditory mode of conducting meetings. Just stand up and grab a marker. Write down each idea or issue that's presented on a self-stick note and slap it on flipchart or banner paper, or better yet, let the team members write down their own ideas, say them out loud, and have them slap them on the paper themselves.

Try affinity diagramming if you are going to generate a lot of ideas and need to get them organized quickly. Looking for root causes? Try the interrelationship digraph tool. Trying to narrow down the list of ideas? Use multivoting. Want to analyze the ideas and select the best one? Then the MT decision matrix will do the trick. All of the team-based tools we discussed will keep the team involved, utilize their knowledge and expertise, and produce the best possible results for the project.

Act as a Facilitator, Not a Director

In the old model of management, the project manager acted like a dictator, deciding what needed to get done, and then handing out assignments to team members. In the new model, the project leader acts as a facilitator. Three of the most important rules for facilitating are: (1) Honor individual differences; (2) Create and maintain a safe environment; (3) Focus on the process and not the content. By facilitating the

223

process, and making sure you have the right people on the team, the content will take care of itself.

Manage the Team Process

All teams evolve through the stages of team development, but not all make it to the highest evolutionary stage—performing. Part of the job of the project leader is to manage the team process so that the team does make it to the performing stage, where people are satisfied with the work they're doing and they're productive and having fun. Managing the team process starts at kick off and continues through close out. Using participative, team-based tools for project management will help to build a team.

Leading both the team process and the project management process requires a whole new set of leadership skills. These include

- ✔ Team skills.
- ✔ Facilitation skills.
- ✔ Conflict-resolution skills and tools.
- ✔ Constructive-feedback skills.
- ✔ Problem-solving tools.
- ✔ Brainstorming tools.
- ✔ Decision-making tools.
- ✔ Communication skills.
- ✔ Project management skills.

KEY 6—COMMUNICATE EFFECTIVELY

Communication is a challenge in any organization, but it's a particular challenge when you're working on a project. A project is like a start-up enterprise. A project is commissioned because something new needs to be developed or something existing needs to be improved. A team is assembled and the customer and stakeholders are identified. Lines of communication must be established. Both internal and external communication procedures must be developed.

Internal communications happen primarily through team meetings, voice mail, and e-mail. The project leader needs to establish a schedule for team meetings. These meetings need to be held using good meeting-management techniques. Effective meetings go a long way to establishing productive lines of communication. In addition, formal information flow between team members and between the project leader and team members should be defined. For example, are status updates due before the team meeting? If so, when?

The most important external communications are those between the project leader and the sponsor and customer. In addition to the interactions that occur in developing and approving the project, the sponsor and customer need ongoing updates on project status and change requests.

In addition, other stakeholders, such as resource managers must be kept informed of progress and their inputs solicited. This is done by team-member liaisons, members of the project team who have been assigned the responsibility of communicating with assigned stakeholders.

Although communication can often seem like a time-consuming exercise, it's hard to have too much communication, particularly when you're working on a project that will result in a change to the organization or something very new. Preparing stakeholders for the results of the project is as important to its success as doing the tasks of the project in the first place.

KEY 7—LEARN FROM YOUR MISTAKES

Maybe the most important key is learning from your mistakes, so you can avoid making the same mistakes in the future. It's also important to learn from your successes, so you can repeat those next time around.

Lessons will be learned and documented during the project. In addition, at the end of the project, it's important to take the time to

225

revisit what happened throughout the project. Get the customer, sponsor, and stakeholders to evaluate the project. What did you do well? What could you improve? Also ask the team members to evaluate the project. What went well? What did they learn?

Once you've documented all the lessons, consider doing a root-cause analysis (interrelationship digraph) of the problems you experienced. This will help you trace back what were some of the most important things that you could have done differently to avoid the problems in the future.

During the project, it's also important to continually solicit feedback from the team and stakeholders about what could be improved. The sooner you know there is a problem, the sooner you can fix it.

What you learned from the project can be translated into templates or checklists for the next project team. Each project team will then learn from the last one, improving the capability of the entire organization to successfully carry out projects.

CONCLUDING

If you employ the seven keys to success by following the CORE PM method, you'll undoubtedly arrive at the Emerald City on most of your projects. However, in spite of your best efforts, some projects will still crash and burn. It's part of the nature of projects, since you're creating something new or improved, sometimes the technology just doesn't work out or the politics in the organization get in the way. Using the tools, tips, and techniques in this book will raise your chances of success significantly. Give it a try. There's only improvement to look forward to.

Appendix

Project Leadership Self-Assessment

ssess your leadership skills with the following self-assessment. Use a 1 to 6 scale:

1 = almost never

2 = once in a while

3 = less than half the time

4 = more than half the time

5 = most of the time

6 = all the time

#	Statement	Rating
1.	I make sure the team creates and follows a team contract.	1 2 3 4 5 6
2.	I have the team use team-based decision-making tools for making decisions quickly and effectively.	1 2 3 4 5 6

#	Statement	Rating
3.	I make sure the team is clear on which decisions are inside and outside the purview of the team.	1 2 3 4 5 6
4.	I record all information exchanged in the team meetings on flip-chart or banner paper.	1 2 3 4 5 6
5.	I create a team environment that is free of fear and blame.	1 2 3 4 5 6
6.	I treat each individual on the team with respect.	1 2 3 4 5 6
7.	I make sure that everyone has an equal opportunity to participate.	1 2 3 4 5 6
8.	When we are brainstorming, I make sure every idea is recorded and that there is no judgment of ideas.	1 2 3 4 5 6
9.	I provide personal constructive feedback (both positive and negative) to team members when needed.	1 2 3 4 5 6
10.	I create a team process that accommodates differences in thinking, processing, and learning styles.	1 2 3 4 5 6
11.	I practice effective listening so I am sure I understand what the other person is saying/feeling.	1 2 3 4 5 6
12.	I ensure that conflicts are resolved with win/win solutions.	1 2 3 4 5 6
13.	I personally recognize achievements by team members.	1 2 3 4 5 6
14.	I am not afraid to be challenged on my ideas.	1 2 3 4 5 6
15.	I can and do learn from the team.	1 2 3 4 5 6
16.	I know how to manage each stage of team development (forming, storming, norming, performing, and mourning).	1 2 3 4 5 6
17.	I lead the team through the four phases of a project management process.	1 2 3 4 5 6
18.	Everyone on the team participates in planning and monitoring the project.	1 2 3 4 5 6

#	Statement	Rating
19.	Everyone on the team is clear about what they are accountable for.	1 2 3 4 5 6
20.	I maintain good relationships with the sponsor and customer.	1 2 3 4 5 6
21.	I have team members evaluate the plus/deltas for each meeting we have.	1 2 3 4 5 6
22.	We periodically celebrate our successes.	1 2 3 4 5 6
23.	I help the team resolve problems before going to the sponsor or the customer for help.	1 2 3 4 5 6
24.	I keep the sponsor and customer informed on the status of the project.	1 2 3 4 5 6
25.	I make sure close out is conducted without finger pointing or blame, so that true learning can occur.	1 2 3 4 5 6

Appendix B

Thinking Styles

There are four main thinking styles: left-brained cerebral, left-brained limbic, right-brained cerebral, and right-brained limbic. To make it easier, let's give each of these types a name, as shown in Table B.1.

Each of these styles brings critical thinking skills to a project team.

ANALYTICAL

Analytical thinkers tend to be logical and fact based. They prefer quantitative data and precision. People who have analytical thinking styles help the project team make logical, well thought-out decisions.

TABLE B.1 Thinking Styles	
Group	*Name*
Left-brained cerebral	Analytical
Left-brained limbic	Sequential
Right-brained cerebral	Holistic
Right-brained limbic	Interpersonal

SEQUENTIAL

Sequential thinkers are good at organizing and planning. They prefer solving problems pragmatically. People with sequential thinking skills help get the team organized and push for implementation. They are naturals at project management.

HOLISTIC

Holistic thinkers are good at seeing the big picture. They prefer exploring new possibilities and ideas. The people with holistic thinking traits help the team brainstorm new ideas, synthesize information, and solve problems intuitively. They help the team get outside the box.

INTERPERSONAL

Interpersonal thinkers are good at creating enthusiasm and maintaining morale in a group. They help move the team through the stages of team formation. People with interpersonal thinking skills promote conciliation, pick up on conflicts, and help to get them resolved, and maintain relationships within the team.

There are 16 specific styles within each of the four categories. Some people's thinking style strengths are concentrated in one category. Other people have strengths in more than one category.

In a team environment, it's important to understand the strengths and weaknesses of the thinking styles of each individual and the group as a whole. For example, if there is a deficit in the analytical category, then the project team leader will need to work harder at making sure that decisions are made with facts and data and not just gut feel. The MT decision matrix tool, discussed in Chapter 11, would be a good analytical tool to use to augment the analytical approach of the group.

The thinking styles of each individual and the team as a whole can be profiled using the *Diversity Game*, developed by Applied Creativity and produced by the Ned Hermann Group. It is available for purchase on the MartinTate web site at www.projectresults.com.

Sample Team Contract

A. COMMITMENTS

As a project team we will

1. Only agree to do work that we are qualified and capable of doing.

2. Be honest and realistic in planning and reporting project scope, schedule, staffing, and cost.

3. Operate in a proactive manner, anticipating potential problems and working to prevent them before they happen.

4. Promptly notify our customer(s) and sponsor of any change that could affect them.

5. Keep other team members informed.

6. Keep proprietary information about our customers in strict confidence.

7. Focus on what is best for the project as a whole.

8. See the project through to completion.

B. TEAM MEETING
GROUND RULES: PARTICIPATION

We will

1. Keep issues that arise in meetings in confidence within the team unless otherwise indicated.

2. Be honest and open during meetings.

3. Encourage a diversity of opinions on all topics.

4. Give everyone the opportunity for equal participation.

5. Be open to new approaches and listen to new ideas.

6. Avoid placing blame when things go wrong. Instead, we will discuss the process and explore how it can be improved.

C. TEAM MEETING
GROUND RULES: COMMUNICATION

We will

1. Seek first to understand, and then to be understood.

2. Be clear and to the point.

3. Practice active, effective listening skills.

4. Keep discussions on track.

5. Use visual means such as drawings, charts, and tables to facilitate discussion.

D. TEAM MEETING GROUND
RULES: PROBLEM SOLVING

We will

1. Encourage everyone to participate.

2. Encourage all ideas (no criticism), because new concepts come from outside of our normal perceptions.

3. Build on each other's ideas.

4. Use team tools when appropriate to facilitate problem solving.

5. Whenever possible, use data to assist in problem solving.

6. Remember that solving problems is a creative process—new ideas and new understandings often result.

E. TEAM MEETING GROUND RULES: DECISION MAKING

We will

1. Make decisions based on data whenever feasible.

2. Seek to find the needed information or data.

3. Discuss criteria (cost, time, impact, and so on) for making a decision before choosing an option.

4. Encourage and explore different interpretations of data.

5. Get input from the entire team before a decision is made.

6. Discuss concerns with other team members during the team meetings or privately rather than with non–team members in inappropriate ways.

7. Ask all team members if they can support a decision before the decision is made.

F. TEAM MEETING GROUND RULES: HANDLING CONFLICT

We will

1. Regard conflict as normal and as an opportunity for growth.

2. Seek to understand the interests and desires of each party involved before arriving at answers or solutions.

235

3. Choose an appropriate time and place to discuss and explore the conflict.

4. Listen openly to other points of view.

5. Repeat back to the other person what we understand and ask if it is correct.

6. Acknowledge valid points that the other person has made.

7. State our points of view and our interests in a nonjudgmental and nonattacking manner.

8. Seek to find some common ground for agreement.

G. MEETING GUIDELINES

1. Meetings will be held every _____ days/weeks/months.

2. Meetings will be called by _____
   _____.

3. Agendas will be issued every _____ days/weeks in advance by _____.

4. Meetings will be facilitated by _____
   _____.

5. Evaluations of meetings will be conducted every _____ meeting.

6. The scribe will issue minutes within _____ days of the meeting.

H. MEETING PROCEDURES

1. Meetings will begin and end on time.

2. Team members will come to the meetings prepared.

3. Pagers and cell phones will be turned off during meetings.

4. Agenda items for the next meeting will be discussed at the end of each meeting.

5. A Parking Lot will be used to capture off-the-subject ideas and concerns.

6. Unresolved issues will be added to the Issues list.

7. If a team member cannot attend a meeting, he or she will send a representative with authority to make decisions.

8. Meeting tasks will be rotated among members.

Signatures: (Team members)

_____

_____

_____

_____

_____

_____

_____

Appendix

MT Problem-Solving Methodology

The MartinTate (MT) Problem-Solving Methodology is called DAS/IR. In the first three stages (DAS), the problem is defined (Define stage), analyzed (Analyze stage) and then a solution is selected (Select stage). The IR stages are used for implementing the solution.

The first three stages are the ones that should be worked through before any major implementation project is initiated.

Stage One—Define the Problem (D). In the first stage, the team studies the problem and the environment in which the problem fits. Any existing data about the problem is studied and a problem statement is written.

Stage Two—Analyze the Problem (A). In the second stage, data is collected to clarify the problem, the process in which the problem exists is mapped, and the root causes of the problem are identified. Finally a cause statement is written.

Stage Three—Select a Solution (S). In the third stage, the team brainstorms possible solutions to the problem and generates

239

several potential solutions. Each solution is then evaluated and the optimal solution is selected. A solution description is written.

This three-stage process should be done before any project that will implement a solution to a perceived problem is initiated. Make sure you've identified the real causes to the presenting problem and the best possible solution before embarking on any implementation project. When the problem definition and solution selection requires a team of people to carry it out, this three-stage problem-solving process becomes a project in and of itself. It should be initiated, planned, executed, and closed out.

The last two stages of the methodology, Implementation and Review (IR), are also a project. During implementation, the team designs and then pilots the solution. If the pilot is successful, the solution is rolled out to the full population. During review, performance data from the solution is compared to the original data collected about the problem, to ensure that the solution will resolve the root causes of the identified problem. If necessary, corrections are made to the solution and then the solution is handed off to the business-process manager who is accountable for ongoing maintenance of the solution.

Project Management Self-Assessment

The following survey will help you assess your project management abilities. Complete the following self-assessment, using a 1 to 6 scale:

1 = almost never

2 = once in a while

3 = less than half the time

4 = more than half the time

5 = most of the time

6 = all of the time

#	Statement	Rating
1.	My projects are completed on time.	1 2 3 4 5 6
2.	My customers are satisfied with the project management process and the final deliverables produced.	1 2 3 4 5 6

#	Statement	Rating
3.	Stakeholders are satisfied with the project management process.	1 2 3 4 5 6
4.	My projects are completed within budget.	1 2 3 4 5 6
5.	I use a participatory project management method when I manage projects.	1 2 3 4 5 6
6.	I never begin a project without a charter.	1 2 3 4 5 6
7.	I hold a participative kick-off meeting to introduce the team to the project.	1 2 3 4 5 6
8.	I make sure that the customer need is well understood.	1 2 3 4 5 6
9.	I make sure that customer requirements are clearly defined.	1 2 3 4 5 6
10.	I make sure the team identifies and manages stakeholder interests.	1 2 3 4 5 6
11.	The team defines the scope boundaries for the project.	1 2 3 4 5 6
12.	A subproject tree, showing clear accountability for subprojects and deliverables, is completed by the team for each project.	1 2 3 4 5 6
13.	A risk assessment is completed for each of my projects, and countermeasures to reduce risk are identified and included in the project plan.	1 2 3 4 5 6
14.	My schedules include a contingency factor for unforeseen problems.	1 2 3 4 5 6
15.	Staff effort requirements are documented in the project plan.	1 2 3 4 5 6
16.	Project plans are reviewed and approved by the sponsor, customer, and key stakeholders.	1 2 3 4 5 6
17.	Change-management procedures are included in each project plan document.	1 2 3 4 5 6
18.	The main project team focuses on deliverables and allows the subprojects to focus on activities.	1 2 3 4 5 6

#	Statement	Rating
19.	Interdependencies are carefully managed at both the main project and subproject levels.	1 2 3 4 5 6
20.	Subproject leaders are empowered to get their pieces of the work done and held accountable for the results.	1 2 3 4 5 6
21.	All project status reports use a standard format.	1 2 3 4 5 6
22.	Staff effort actuals are documented on the status report form.	1 2 3 4 5 6
23.	Project teams perform customer evaluations as part of the close-out process.	1 2 3 4 5 6
24.	Lessons learned and recommendations for improvement are included in the close-out report.	1 2 3 4 5 6

Glossary

Accountability   To ensure that a result is achieved, usually through the effort of others.

Accuracy rating   A high, medium, or low rating that depicts the level of confidence the team has in an estimate.

Ad hoc member   Attendance at team meetings is by invitation only.

Affinity diagram   A team-based tool for identifying and organizing ideas.

Assumption   Something that is believed to be true.

Auditory learner   Someone who learns best by talking, discussing, or listening.

Brainstorming   A process for generating ideas.

Budget   The amount of staff-effort time and/or money approved for a project.

Budget risk   The potential problems that could cause the team to overspend the budget.

Business case   The reasons that the project has been authorized. How the project ties into the strategic goals of the organization.

Business process   A set of steps that turns inputs into repetitive outputs. One of the ways, besides projects, that work is accomplished.

Change log   The means by which a project leader tracks the status of change requests.

Change management   A structured process for making changes to the project plan.

Change request   A request from inside or outside the project to amend the project plan.

Charter   The output of the initiation phase. It outlines the expectations and constraints that the team will use when they plan the project.

Close-out phase   The final project management phase in which the project is evaluated, feedback is elicited, and lessons learned are captured.

Close-out report   The output of the close-out phase. It includes the final status report, evaluation and feedback documents, lessons learned, and recommendations for improving the project system.

Consensus   Agreement within a group that everyone can live with a decision.

Constraint   Something that the team is not allowed to do or resources that are not available to the project.

Contingency   Reserve resources (time, effort, or money) that are set aside because of the unpredictability of the future.

CORE PM™   A participative, team-based method for managing any project. The CORE Project Management™ method was developed by MartinTate.

Cost risk   The same as budget risk. The potential problems that could cause the team to overspend the budget.

Countermeasure   An activity or deliverable that will prevent or reduce a risk.

Criteria   The factors used to make a decision.

Critical path   The path through the schedule in which there is no slack. The critical path is the longest path through the schedule and it determines the final delivery date in the project.

Customer acceptance criteria   The criteria the customer will use to determine if he or she is satisfied with the final deliverable.

Customer evaluation   An assessment by the customer, after the final deliverable has been delivered, of his or her level of satisfaction with the project.

Customer need   The problem that the final deliverable will help the customer resolve.

Customer requirements   Specific features or functions that the customer wants from the final deliverable.

Deadline   The date for delivery of a deliverable that is set by someone outside the project team, usually the sponsor or customer.

Decision options   The choices available before a final decision is made.

Deliverable   An output from the technical process of the project.

Deliverables schedule   The schedule that shows the delivery date for each of the project's deliverables and the interdependencies between them.

Deliverables staff effort   The internal effort required to create the deliverables for the project.

Delivery date   The date a deliverable is scheduled to be turned over to the next customer in the technical process.

Directive project management   The old management approach in which the project manager did the planning, delegated tasks to team members, monitored the project, and then shut it down.

Duration   The calendar time required to complete a deliverable or activity.

Empowerment   The act of pushing decision making down to the lowest level possible. The opposite of micromanagement.

End customer   The customer that will ultimately use the product or service being developed. The end user.

End user   The person(s) who uses a product, service, or process.

End-user requirements   The performance characteristics of the final product, service, or process that are requested by the end user.

Execution phase   The phase in the project management process in which the deliverables are created and their progress is tracked.

Executive summary   A short overview written for senior management.

Expectations   What the customer is hoping will be accomplished.

External costs Expenses for the project that originate outside the organization.

External customer A customer who resides outside the organization.

Facilitation The act of helping a person or group to work through a process.

Features Specific attributes of final deliverables.

Final deliverable The final output from the execution phase of the project that is delivered to the project customer.

Final status report The last status report for the project, completed after the project customer has accepted the final deliverable.

Forming stage The first stage of team development. It is when people are getting to know one another.

Functional manager The person accountable for a department or a set of resources. Also known as a resource manager.

Gantt chart A schedule that visually shows the duration for each deliverable or activity.

Historical data Data collected from past projects.

Icebreaker A tool that is used to help people feel more comfortable in a group.

Impact analysis The assessment of what effect something will have on the project plan.

Initial team The team originally selected to be on the project.

Initiation The first project management phase. In this phase the overall direction and constraints for the project are set.

Input A supply that is used in a process.

Input/output chain The workflow of interconnected or interdependent deliverables that creates the final deliverable.

Interdependencies The dependencies that exist in any system, where one team member depends on another for certain inputs or to receive certain outputs.

Interim deliverable   A deliverable that is produced in the technical process before the production of the final deliverable.

Internal costs   Expenses for the project that are cross-charged by a department inside the organization.

Internal customer   A customer that is inside the organization.

Interrelationship digraph   A team-based tool that helps a team identify root causes.

Issues list   A list to record issues that must be resolved or action items that are not significant enough to put on the project schedule.

Kick off   Typically the first meeting of the project team, when the project is officially launched.

Kinesthetic learners   People who learn best by doing or sensing.

Large project   A project with more than ten team members.

Lessons-learned list   The compilation of what has been learned during a project as a result of both successes and failures.

Liaison   A person on the project team assigned to communicate with a stakeholder.

Method   A system for getting something done.

Milestone   A major accomplishment of the project.

Milestone schedule   The schedule used to communicate the dates that major accomplishments in the project will be completed.

Mourning stage   The last stage in the team-development process.

MT Decision matrix   A team-based tool that helps a team analyze and select a decision out of multiple options.

Multivoting   A team-based tool for selecting one or more options for a decision.

Norming stage   The third stage in Tuckman's stages of team development. Typically each person has accepted accountability to get his or her work done.

Output   A product that is produced as a result of a process.

Oversight The act of high-level monitoring to assure that a project is on track.

Parking lot A meeting-management tool that provides a place to collect ideas or concerns that are not part of the immediate discussion.

Participative project management The new approach to managing a project in which the team collaborates with the project leader to create a project plan, monitor and track the project, and close down the project.

Performing stage The fourth stage in Tuckman's stages of team development. In this stage the team reaches optimal performance with team members supporting one another to accomplish the goals of the project.

Phase A set of activities within the project management process.

Phase gate Go/no go decision points at the end of each project management phase.

PI matrix A grid diagram used to organize risk self-stick notes according to their probabilities and impacts.

Plan A document that describes how something should be accomplished.

Planning phase The second phase of the project management process in which a plan for how the project will be executed is developed and approved.

Plus/delta form A form that allows teams to capture what went well and ideas for improvement.

Predecessor A deliverable or activity that must be done before the next deliverable or activity can be completed.

Process A set of steps that transforms an input(s) into an output(s).

Product A tangible or intangible good produced via a process.

Project A temporary endeavor that produces a unique output.

Project leader The person who leads the project team through the four phases of a project.

Project management   The application of knowledge, skills, tools, and techniques to meet or exceed customer expectations from a project.

Project management staff effort   The amount of time that people on the project team will spend in project management activities such as attending meetings, writing reports, planning, and so on.

Project objectives   The purpose of the project. The significant accomplishments that the project must achieve.

Project plan   A complete plan for how the project will be executed. The output of the planning phase.

Project priorities   The ranking of the triple constraints for the project—scope versus schedule versus budget.

Project team members   The people on the main project team.

Range   A numerical spread from lowest to highest. This is typically used to represent the staff effort and spending estimate numbers.

Resource managers   Also known as functional managers. They provide the resources, primarily the people, to work on the project.

Resource planning   The plan for who will be involved in the project, how much time it will take, and what it will cost.

Rework   Doing the work over because the work was not done right the first time.

Risk assessment   The process of identifying, analyzing, and preventing risks from occurring.

Risk identification   The process of brainstorming what potential problems might occur in the project.

Risk impact   The effect the risk would have on the project if it occurred.

Risk probability   The likelihood that the risk will occur.

Risk rating   The level of risk that the team determines is in the project.

Risks   The potential problems that could arise in the project.

Schedule The dates of completion for deliverables or activities mapped against the project's timelines.

Schedule risk The potential problems that could occur that would prevent the team from meeting its deadline dates.

Scope The definition of what will be produced by the project for the customer.

Scope boundaries The fence that is placed around the scope of the project to delineate what is inside and outside the project scope.

Scope description A written explanation of features and functions of the final deliverable.

Scope plan The part of the project plan that relates to scope. It includes the scope description of the final deliverable, customer acceptance criteria, scope boundaries, and a stakeholder list.

Scope risk Potential problems that could prevent the team from meeting the customer's acceptance criteria.

Service The act of one person doing for another.

Slack time Free time that exists between the completion of a predecessor and the start of a successor.

Small project A project with ten or fewer team members.

Software scheduling program Any software program that can be used to transfer the deliverables schedule into electronic form.

Spending budget The approved spending estimate.

Spending estimate The projected costs of the project.

Spending limit The maximum amount of money that can be spent on the project.

Sponsor The person who acts as a liaison between the project leader and the management team, providing oversight to the project.

Sponsor evaluation The evaluation of the project by the sponsor.

Staff effort The amount of time people inside the organization will spend on the project.

Staff-effort budget The approved staff-effort estimate.

Staff-effort costs   The dollar rate for each person or subproject multiplied by the staff-effort estimate for that person or subproject.

Staff-effort estimate   The projected amount of time that each person or subproject will need to spend to complete the project.

Staff-effort limit   The maximum amount of time people inside the organization can spend working on the project.

Stage gates   Go/no go decision points within the technical process for a project.

Stakeholders   Any person or group affected by the project.

Status report   Reports issued during the execution phase of the project that denote if the project is on track or not.

Storming stage   The second of Tuckman's stages of team development. At this stage, conflicts about what will be done and who will do it arise in the team.

Subproject   A subsection of the main project responsible for producing a set of deliverables.

Subproject leader   The person who leads the subproject team through the project management process.

Subproject team   The group of people who complete the work of a subproject.

Subproject tree   The organizational chart for the project that shows subprojects, deliverables within each subproject, and accountability for each subproject.

Successor   A deliverable that comes immediately after a predecessor deliverable.

Team contract   An agreement developed by the team that defines the guidelines that the team will follow as they work together as a team.

Team process   The process that helps the team work through the stages of team development.

Team-based tools   Tools that are specifically designed to enhance team participation and that incorporate the three different sensory learning styles: auditory, visual, and kinesthetic.

Technical process   The specific process used to produce the deliverables. For example, in a software project, the technical process is the software development process. The technical process is specific to the deliverables being produced and is distinct from the generic project management process.

Timeline   A length of the entire project, broken down into days, weeks, or months.

Total quality   The management technology that addresses customer focus, prevention, and assurance of quality.

Tracking project progress   The act of determining if the project is on track to meet the commitments outlined in the project plan.

Triple constraint   The three interdependent variables in a project: scope, schedule, and cost.

Variance   The difference between what actually occurred and what was planned or projected to occur.

Visual learners   People who learn best through visual data such as written documents, graphs, pictures, and so on.

Work process   A set of steps that produces an output or deliverable.

Write it! Say it! Slap it!   A brainstorming method developed by MartinTate. Team members write their ideas on self-stick notes, say them out loud, and slap them on flip-chart or banner paper that has been taped to the wall.

Index